Pablo Valdivia

Spanish Literature, Crisis and Spectrality: Notes on a Haunted Canon

Hispanic Transnational Studies

edited by

Prof. Dr. Pablo Valdivia
(University of Groningen)

volume 2

LIT

Pablo Valdivia

Spanish Literature, Crisis and Spectrality: Notes on a Haunted Canon

LIT

Cover image:
https://pixabay.com/es/esp%C3%ADritu-creepy-halloween-fantasma-2304469/
Public Domain Picture

This project has received funding from the European Union's Horizon 2020 research and innovation programme under the Marie Skłodowska-Curie grant agreement No 645666

Bibliographic information published by the Deutsche Nationalbibliothek
The Deutsche Nationalbibliothek lists this publication in the Deutsche Nationalbibliografie; detailed bibliographic data are available on the Internet at http://dnb.d-nb.de.

ISBN 978-3-643-90573-4 (pb)
ISBN 978-3-643-95573-9 (PDF)

A catalogue record for this book is available from the British Library

Klosbachstr. 107
CH-8032 Zürich
Tel. +41 (0) 44-251 75 05
E-Mail: zuerich@lit-verlag.ch http://www.lit-verlag.ch
Distribution:
In the UK: Global Book Marketing, e-mail: mo@centralbooks.com
In North America: International Specialized Book Services, e-mail: orders@isbs.com
In Germany: LIT Verlag Fresnostr. 2, D-48159 Münster
Tel. +49 (0) 2 51-620 32 22, Fax +49 (0) 2 51-922 60 99, e-mail: vertrieb@lit-verlag.de

e-books are available at www.litwebshop.de

Table of Contents

Introduction: literature, crisis and a spectre in Lima[1]

José Ricardo Morales taught me to believe in the unpredictable. He used to say: 'there is no life without a project'. And a new project, thus a new life, came to me when I was about to finish the writing up of this book.[2] The University of Groningen gave me the once-in-a-life opportunity to create my department, choose my team, get the resources and support I needed for building my dreamed program. Therefore, from June 2016, I started in my new position as Chair and Full Professor of European Culture and Literature at the University of Groningen.

Today, in Lima, below the spectral quietness and solitude of my lovely Miraflores apartment and the warmth of early January summer of 2018, I write these lines while I contemplate in the distance of my terrace the ruins of the Huaca Pucllana. Semi-hidden, thanks to the kindness of the colleagues from the Pontificia Universidad Católica del Perú (my gratitude to Gisela Canepa), the Universidad Nacional San Marcos and the European Commission, I enjoy my days in Lima under one-month research stay planned to finish the writing up of this book and other delayed projects.

I must confess it feels extraordinarily strange to have time for me finally. It seems somehow unreal to freely go for a walk, read anything I want, devote hours to think, enjoy my cooking or take a nap, without the Damocles sword of the committee's deadlines and the usual extra-work which entails setting up something new from scratch.

[1] This book has received funding from the European Union's Horizon 2020 research and innovation programme under the Marie Skłodowska-Curie grant agreement No 645666.

[2] Also, I would like to thank Margareth van Hezik who helped me with the editing in an early stage of this book.

Slowing down the rush of the last 18 months produces a sort of vertigo challenging to handle. In fact, I am astonished of everything that has happened after I put into motion the crazy idea of building up a top class international teaching and research program in Groningen. Everybody thought I was out of my mind and it was utterly pretentious trying to achieve the goal of setting a world-class program in 5 years time. Unexpectedly, instead of 5 years, we only needed 12 months to reach our goals. And, surprisingly, a growing legend about our department is establishing us as the Groningen School of Critical Theory (despite we still have the functional name of Program of European Languages and Cultures) and one of the finest and more active research groups in international academia.

While I write, most of the members of my team are traveling the world and offering essential contributions in the fields of the Humanities and Social Sciences. January is our research month, and we have received so many invitations from so many different countries that we, accordingly, had to adjust our involvement. Back home, in Groningen, increasing numbers of students make the situation even more challenging: we have grown so fast that we have turned into a highly selective programme without seeking it on purpose.

Many enthusiast colleagues ask us what our secret is? However, I could not reduce our work to a little equation. What I believe it makes Groningen unique is the fact we have all the conditions needed to be innovative. In the last months, I have dragged my team into the craziest experiments: introducing artificial intelligence for the study of literature, applying machine learning to improve our student's analytical skills and defying traditional logic in teaching and researching, especially what I consider empty theoretical speculation. Perhaps the only secret is in a simple fact that we indeed work as a team. In this regard, we resemble more a laboratory of committed scientists that the traditional humanities department where strong individualism rarely allows teamwork to flourish.

Therefore, I would like to thank all my colleagues and especially Vera Alexander, Alberto Godioli, Florian Lippert, Konstantin Mierau, Camilla Sutherland, Lars Rensmann and Stefan Couperus for being my initial accomplices in this adventure. It is so fulfilling and one of the greatest gifts to know that I can knock at any time on their doors, share with them any of my friendly 'world domination plans' and turn them real. Also, I would like to name here three excellent colleagues, and friends, whose support was vital, to begin with, the Groningen endeavor: Antonio Sánchez Jiménez, Yolanda Rodríguez Pérez, and Manuel de la Fuente. Their kindness can only be compared with the high quality of their academic work.

While most departments in Humanities research on spotting tinier and tinier differences (if not inventing them), we subverted academic fashions and mainstream academia by addressing research problems in their radical specificity and their universal agency. In this sense, we feel heirs of the noblest Enlightenment (yes, I know some readers will start at this point with the mantra of my alleged Eurocentrism) as we believe in an aspiration for a world with no nationalism, with no passports, with no assassin differences.

Nationalisms have managed to put the Humanities and the Social Sciences to the rear of social innovation and engineering. It is the moment to bring back the Humanities, especially Literary Studies, to the forefront avantgarde of academic research as we are the only disciplinary scholars trained to make the questions nobody dares to ask, to provide the analytical and creative skills that 'dataism' and growing 'technolatry' are displacing. We are the last line of humanist resistance before the dataist theology of the 21st Century. Is this meaning I reject technological innovations? No, algorithms and machine learning are here to stay, but it has to be under our own rules. Rules which are not written yet, applied uses of the new probabilities world borning now. Ignoring what is at stake would be irresponsible. Mastering the latest technologies is our duty as humanists. My book finishes pointing in that direction.

Also, this volume is a contribution, in English and Spanish, to the conflictive relationship between literature and crisis. And, in this regard, it tackles critical problems for the understanding of institutional canonicity, historical consciousness and power constructions of cultural imaginaries. This book comprises a range of texts which orbit around the notional hypothesis that literature is the only human discourse that masters all the remaining discourses. In other words, using an algorithmic metaphor, Literature is the algorithm that masters all discourses. Therefore, by studying the spectral nature of the works, authors and problems offered in this volume, we will be able to better understand why the study of the Spanish literature of the 20th and 21st is embedded in a historiographical anomaly and how it can be solved if we throw away our old lenses and we use transnational glasses.

I have written these lines during the sun rising in Lima. I am a spectre in a city where nobody knows me. I live in between cultures, countries, and disciplines. Yesterday somebody asked me what was my specialization within the Peruvian literature without noticing that there is an initial structural mistake in that assertion. There is no Peruvian, or Spanish, or English, or French literature. I adore César Vallejo's writing in a sense his work appeals cultural universals that can be shared and experienced from Japan to Chile, from Russia to New Zealand. Topics and themes are universal, and their specific representation is historical, not even nationally based. The nation is dead but some politicians are so blind that cannot see what is coming, what is already here to some extent: technology overcoming nation-based principles. But of course, this topic goes beyond the boundaries and scope of the present book, and it will have to be addressed in my next monograph study.

Finally, I would like to express my gratitude for their support and endless help to Bonifacio Valdivia, Carmen Martín, Víctor Valdivia and Gema Ocaña who made me the person I am. All my work, all my efforts, all my successes belong to them. *Concordia res parvae crescent.*

1. Threshold: Albert Kahn and Jacques Derrida in a haunted hall of residence

As one of my favorite filmmakers, Alfred Hitchcock, used to say: 'Ideas come from everything'. So did the idea of writing this book. The initial plan of this study came to me in different moments over the last fourteen years summarized in three particular stages.

The first stage took place when I was a Ph.D. student at the University of Nottingham. In those times, I was also a tutor in a Hall of Residence, Willoughby Hall, based on campus. Many nights I was on duty, which meant that I had to deal with students' emergencies and stay awake until the day porter arrived. To be honest, only very few incidents concerned serious matters, and there was plenty of time at night to work, read and watch movies. The Hall was a sort of haunted house in which errant drunk students acted as ghosts: they were spectres whose nights' actions only were present the morning after. To illustrate such mysteries of nature, I might friendly refer to how once, a tree —close to the entrance of Willoughby Hall— was found decorated with six bicycles at the top branches one early morning. Or on another remarkable occasion, a very heavy iron bench from a nearby park lurked in its solitude in a middle of the third-floor corridor when the first cleaners started their turn. Therefore, one can conclude that during the nights at Willoughby Hall, I had witnessed a secret life —not only of drunken miracles— but also a stimulating one from an anthropological point of view.

Indeed, the Hall of Residence was a haunted house in which anything seemed possible in physical —the reader might indulge my irony— and also in intellectual terms. In my particular case, I had hours ahead and the necessary means to spend my time enjoying the pleasures of reading and researching alone with no management or more mundane preoccupations that could refrain me from doing what I loved to do.

Therefore, I experienced a kind of intellectual freedom that I have decided to recover for this book, and especially for this prologue as the reader might already have noticed from the specific tone chosen for my writing.

Thus, in the atmosphere of freedom present in Willoughby Hall (for which my thanks to the genius of its former warden Professor Bernard J. McGuirk, whose mastery has greatly influenced my academic work) I, during one of my 'on duty nights', had the chance of watching a documentary film broadcast by the BBC which was about a man entirely unfamiliar to me at the time: Albert Kahn.

Albert Kahn (1860-1940) remains an unknown figure in the Hispanic world. He was a French banker and philanthropist who created an immense project for recording and photographing the world of his days. The project was called *The Archives of the Planet*. It took place over a period of 22 years and resulted in a collection of 72.000 color images and 183.000 meters of film. Albert was the eldest of four children (Okuefuna, 2008). His father was a Jewish cattle dealer and his mother an uneducated homebound woman who died while Albert was still little. They lived in Marmoutier in the Bas-Rhin Alsace in north-eastern France. After the German annexation of the Alsace-Lorraine in 1871, the family moved to Saint-Michel. He became a bank clerk in Paris (1879) and continued his studies with a private tutor: the French philosopher Henri Bergson. Eventually, they forged an extraordinary friendship. In 1892 Albert Kahn was appointed as the principal associate of the Goudchaux Bank, which was, at the time, one of the most influential financial houses of Europe. Then Kahn devoted part of his fortune to the creation of traveling scholarships and the improvement of education. Besides that, he conceived *The Archives of the Planet* project, which was an attempt to apprehend a fading world that would be erased by the two great wars later on. Albert Kahn died at Boulogne-Billancourt in 1940 during the German occupation of France, where he created his *Garden of the Worlds* as a utopian desire for reconciling the world in the form of a botanic garden in which cultures from all over the world could live in harmony.

That night, when I discovered Albert Kahn's attempt to record the Earth visually, two particular aspects fascinated me: the first was an autochrome from *The Archives of the Planet* project in which London was a kind of phantasmagorical set. Fleet Street, in 1924, was empty except for the presence of a man with his back to the camera peering through a shop window. He was present and absent at the same time. His materiality was fragile as his shape blurred. He had no shadow resembling a spectre. A little bit further on, in the same autochrome, colors had even become more blurred and a car, or the illusion of a car, seemed to be driving towards the spectator. In the right side of the image, there were some blackish smoky stains at the corner of a building that resembled a human figure in the movement like if he/she was evaporating or vanishing before our very eyes.

The explanation for these ghostly images offered by Kahn's photographs resides in the limitations of autochrome technique. The Autochrome Lumière was an early photography process patented in 1903 by the Lumière brothers. The autochrome created a kind of pointillist effect that resembled a dream-like impressionist painting. Since I have discovered it, I extensively looked for Albert Kahn's pictures, and I have always found in them a certain sense of fragility and an eerie reality that reminded me History is nothing but a cultural narrative constructed over spectral fictions, communities, and people, revealed to us by blurred forms.

The second aspect that caused my fascination was the fact that Albert Kahn suffered displacement and forced exile due to the German annexation of Alsace. In this sense, Kahn experienced the expulsion, which consolidated his doubled condition of a displaced subject: an individual deprived of his homeland by the German seize of territory and a Jew who was an object of virulent anti-Semitism. Such doubled displaced condition left him in a no man's land. However, although he was forced to move from his original home-village —instead of becoming radicalized and nationalist—, Kahn developed more and more universalist views and positions. For him, what had happened in Alsace, was a symptom of a global process where a fading world was replaced by a new violent reality that erased cultural diversity. Thus, he felt he had the duty to record that fading world before it was too late. Then, from his outlandish double condition, he created *The Archives of the Planet*. Kahn's position was unusual rather than focusing on the justification of a radical self or the promotion of a Herderian's *Volksgeist* which were the two mainstream positions, in ideological terms, at the turn of the century in Europe.

Since that night I referred to before —when I was watching the mentioned BBC documentary film— Albert Kahn has been, in one way or another, present in most of my academic works both with his universalist and humanist example, as some kind of revenant that reminded me of the best achievements of the French encyclopaedism. Universal and humanist values crystallize in that incomplete, vast and overwhelming attempt to visually record the fading world of the turn of the century.

The second stage took place when my Ph.D. supervisor, Professor Bernard J. McGuirk —who studied and collaborated with the French philosopher Jacques Derrida— advised me to read *Specters of Marx* (1993). Derrida had a considerable influence in my department and, subsequently, in the community of 50 Ph.D. students, I belonged. I remember reading Derrida's *Specters of Marx* across several haunted nights in Willoughby Hall. In his book, I found genuinely revealing his assessment of Marx's ideas and his articulation of the resistance against the intolerance performed by late capitalist ideological practices. Furthermore, Derrida taught us how to base any cultural analysis in a double movement: from inside and outside the object of study (Derrida, 1995). Such strategic reading was especially appealing to me when confronting problems related to canonicity and how, as my investigations on Federico García Lorca soon proved, a national canon is never an innocent construction but neither the result of a conspiracy. It always embodies not only didactic purposes but also power and political strategies to justify the hegemony of particular sets of ideas and interests, and it is also the result of luck, human stupidity, and misreading. As Professor David T. Gies explained in his introduction to *The Cambridge History of Spanish Literature* (2005), a literary canon is nothing but a useful fiction.

Although I do not consider myself a Marxist and I am unsure about the possibilities of Marxist ideas to produce an adequate response against the hegemonic hybridization of private capital and state power, I still admire in Marx's philosophy his capacity of analysis to reveal contradictions otherwise naturalized by dominant capitalist ideologies.

Therefore, when coming to deal with the Spanish Peninsular Canon, Marx's ideas still are —through the glasses of Derrida— valuable tools for studying the anomaly, in cultural terms, produced by thirty-five years of Francoist dictatorship (1940-1975). For decades, the Spanish Peninsular Canon presented a disjoint between the literary production of the Republican Exile and the official literature promoted by Francoism: the Spanish Literary Canon is nothing but a net resulted from power and cultural discursive clashes.

The problematic nature of the Spanish 20th Century Literary Canon is rooted in a manipulated historiography of Spanish letters. Such manipulation was created and sustained by the Francoist academia. Surprisingly, despite the advent of democratic times, the Francoist narratives produced to establish the Spanish national canon still are at the base of many textbooks used in secondary schools and university programmes in Spain.

Derrida, of course, never problematized the Spanish 20th Century Literary Canon, but I found in his assessment of the disjoints produced by capitalist power, a helpful insight to the process of canonization forged during Francoist and democratic times in Spain. Recently, in the *Historia de la Literatura Española Volumen 6 Modernidad y Nacionalismo (1900-1939)* —written by Professor José Carlos Mainer and published by Crítica in 2010— Mainer defined the Spanish 20th Century Canon as an anomaly which resulted from the political appropriation of cultural practices for power purposes (Mainer, 2010).

In this regard, the studies of the GEXEL group, based at the Universidad Autónoma de Barcelona, and especially Professor Manuel Aznar Soler, have proved that the recuperation of the Republican Exile has systematically been excluded from the political agenda of Spanish parties, because it has become an uncomfortable issue for politicians and elites (Aznar Soler, 2002). In other words, to recover the works of the Republican Exiles would mean to regain the memory of the Spaniards who suffered the French concentrations camps, who were exterminated by the Nazi Germans and who had to live in ostracism as invisible members of a spectral republic of letters during the post-war times. Specifically, I refer to a spectral republic of letters created by the lack of open channels for the Republicans to get their works published in Spain, to be known and recognized in this country during Francoist times. Francoist censorship, but also biased power interests during democratic years, hurdled the realization of an integral plan for rehabilitation and normalization of the Republican exiles and their cultural achievements.

With reference to this, Derrida's notion of 'Hauntology' became a traveller companion in my search for answers on how to create a comprehensive narrative that could reveal the complexities and contradictions created by the military coup d'état of 1936 and the subsequent dismantle of the 1900-1936

Spanish cultural system, also labelled by critics, as the Silver Age of the Spanish Letters.

The term 'Hauntology' has been criticised by Jürgen Habermas and Richard Rorty. It is not my intention here to historicize the criticism on this notion but to explain why it produced a certain revelation to me when I had to assess problems which had risen by the building up of national canon narratives. Also, I found the term 'Hauntology' quite useful for establishing the foundations of this book. For Derrida, the notion of 'Hauntology' shows us that the present only exists concerning the past. The initial conceptualization of Derrida is in connection with the philosophy of history and the paradoxical nature of the spectre, which is neither being nor non-being. Exiles, as occurs in several cases present in this book, are constructed narratives that could only exist in connection to the past in one way or another.

I will come back to Derrida in several parts of this book but, for the purpose of this threshold-chapter, the reader must understand that despite the efforts of Professor Manuel Aznar Soler, among others, in his fundamental work 'Las Historias de las Literaturas del Exilio Republicano Español de 1939: Problemas Teóricos y Metodológicos' (2002), the central attempts to produce a clear assessment of the Spanish exile of 1939 orbited around the idea of reintegrating exile symbols that were politically convenient or just considering the Spanish exile as an autonomous cultural system.

From my perspective, both approaches were, and are, quite problematic. Firstly, because admitting the validity of the Spanish National Canon without problematizing it, would be equal to accepting it as a useful and innocent tool. Conversely, decades of studies have demonstrated the Francoism created an anomaly as tragically explained by Max Aub in his 'Teatro Español Sacado a la Luz de las Tinieblas de Nuestro Tiempo' (speech fictionally read before the Spanish Academy of Language in 1956), when he named an Academy full of spectral writers killed or forced to exile by the authoritarian rule of General Franco (Aub, 1972). Secondly, because assuring Spanish exile was an autonomous cultural system would be equal to forgetting that Spanish exiles were writing far away from Spain and in most cases, they had no readers or public and they never constituted a single homogenous body. For instance, I just need to name three famous exiles: Francisco Ayala, Max Aub, and José Ricardo Morales. They experienced the exile but under very different circumstances and, consequently, they built up very divergent biographies and literary careers too.

In other words, any scholar studying the Spanish Exile of 1939 should not be tempted to explain it from a single view. It is a subject that rises very complicated questions and, subsequently, it should be solved with a transparency that not excludes complexity in its answers. Derrida made me understand that, to assess the Spanish exile of 1939, we needed new historiographic categories. Accordingly, Derrida, next to Kahn, became another inhabitant of my haunted nights.

Thereby, I focused my efforts to the search of a new historiographic notion that could explain the existence and non-existence at the same time of authors and works in diverse literary systems, worlds of cultural references in disjoint. Moreover, I needed to articulate a satisfactory explanation of complex processes of inclusion and exclusion, center and periphery; and not only of authors but also regarding different works written by the same author. One of the paradigmatic cases of this phenomenon was Antonio Machado whose Republican ideas and vigorous defense of democratic forms resulted in his death under miserable conditions in France. However, one of his works, *Campos de Castilla* (1912), was soon recovered during the decade of the forties by the members of the Francoist intellectual journal *Escorial*. In this journal, Machado was presented as a falangist who chose the wrong side during the Spanish Civil War. Consequently, Machado's

Campos de Castilla was soon included in the Francoist Canon, his texts were studied and printed and Machado was rehabilitated to a vital extent but, I insist, as a nationalist Spanish author which resulted in a total distortion of where his writings and public political engagement had led him to during Republican years.

This particular example, among others, was the object of analysis in my postdoctoral thesis, also written in Nottingham, on post-war Spanish poetry and titled *If it fits it is okay: an Introduction to Postwar Spanish Poetry*. Some of my findings were published in the volume *Literatura y compromiso: Federico García Lorca y Miguel Hernández* (2011) where, under the title 'La recepción crítica del proyecto artístico y ético de Federico García Lorca: hacia una reelaboración de la historia literaria del siglo XX', I explained the dialectics of presence and absence, inclusion, and exclusion performed by Francoist academia during the forties in Spain. Lorca was a spectre for fascists writers: his death was used by the Francoists as a victim that symbolised the supposed violent disorder generated by the Spanish Republic (there are recorded testimonies of writers like Luis Rosales who argued in the '60s that Lorca actually was a full supporter of military dictatorships as forms of government) and his works were cannibalized by many of these writers who took Lorca's writings as aesthetic points of reference or directly plagiarised as it is possible to perceive in the pages of the literary journal *Garcilaso* (1943-1946).

The third stage of this work in progress took place when, while preparing my edition of *Sefarad* (2013) written by Muñoz Molina, I read *The Disinherited: Exile and Making of Spanish Culture 1492-1975* by the historian Henry Kamen (2007). This book obtained great reviews in UK and USA, but I found a suspicious silence around it in Spain. After reading few pages, I immediately understood why. In his remarkable study, Kamen explains how the History of Spain is nothing but series of successive expulsions, exiles and attempts to physically and intellectually annihilate the Other. Every single century in Spanish History has had its great exile. The Francoism epitomised the capacity to murder and force into exile thousands of individuals for ethnic, religious or political reasons and recently accounted in another essential reading *The Spanish Holocaust: inquisition and extermination in twentieth-century Spain* by Paul Preston, published in 2012.

Accordingly, I was not surprised to note why in Spain Kamen's book had received so little attention. In my edition of *Sefarad* (2013), I explained that the map of all possible exiles deployed by Muñoz Molina was the result of an artistic and intellectual gap. On the one hand, Muñoz Molina experienced not having open access to the most critical European post-Second World War literature, which was based on the memory of the Holocaust. It is important to note that recovering that European tradition would have meant improving the memory of the Republican Exile too. Besides the natural dialogue that writers and public should have maintained with the literary representatives of the cultural democracy, such us Max Aub, García Lorca or José Ricardo Morales, never took place. The Francoism interrupted or disjointed such inter-generational natural dialogue.

In this regard, Morales always reminds readers in his smart essays on the Republican Exile of the fact that after 1939 there were only three possible states for those who vindicated a democratic culture: 'enterrado' (dead), 'desterrado' (exiled) or 'aterrado' (terrified, meaning excluded from any possibility of agency in the Spanish public sphere during the years of the dictatorship). Thus, the reader might find Muñoz Molina's speech of 1996 in front of the Spanish Royal Academy of Language, titled as 'Destierro y destiempo de Max Aub', useful. The respondent to his speech was another exile: Francisco Ayala.

And finally, at this third stage, I found the motivation for writing this book when I had the fortune of meeting Professor

Esther Peeren at the University of Amsterdam where I arrived, after years of haunted nights in Willoughby Hall, to fill the position of Lecturer of Hispanic Literature.

Professor Peeren has produced, in my opinion, the two most valuable volumes (one of them in collaboration with María del Pilar Blanco) related to the notion of Spectrality. The first book I would like to refer to is *The Spectralities Reader: ghosts and haunting in contemporary cultural theory* (2013) edited by María del Pilar Blanco and Esther Peeren, which is an excellent tool to any researcher interested in the so-called 'Spectral Turn' (introduced by Roger Luckhurst in 2002). The second book, titled *The Spectral Metaphor: Living Ghosts and the Agency of Invisibility* (2014) is an excellent, inspiring monograph written by Esther Peeren, which explores the spectre as a form of alterity that makes it possible to expose the invisible, more specifically, diverse modes of invisibility: from exploited subjects or marginalized practices to different kinds of dispossession.

Professor Peeren gave me the analytical key I was missing since I had first started working on the Spanish Republican Exile of 1939 and I first viewed exiles, like Albert Kahn, as fragile ghosts living in the disjointed times of two worlds: their countries of origin and the exile's reality. Listening to Peeren's talks, reading her books and discussing with her some particular issues related to my interest on exile writings, made me understand that in order to produce an analysis of the Spanish exile, we needed to see exiles not as historical figures in the traditional sense, but as spectres whose time and public were out of joint. In other words, the spectral metaphor could also be used as a historiographic notion to successfully explain the dialectics of being and not being, having and not having the public in two cultural worlds at the same time. Accordingly, I found of great interest for my research, Peeren's following words: 'First, there is the invocation of the ghost as a figure of return, capable of expressing the persistence of the past in the present and the general workings of repetition as inevitably combining sameness and difference; the ghost, after all, is never identical to who it was when still alive. Second, there is the appeal to the ghost as a present absence: despite being ephemeral, something is *there* that matters and has to be taken into account. It makes possible to consider the social, political, ethical, psychic and affective impacts of "reknowing" or "unforgetting" phenomena previously overlooked or unprocessed, ranging from the empty spaces in buildings to personal or national traumas. Approached through the concept of spectrality, these aspects are not made present in a straightforward manner but manifest in and as their absence, so that their escaping notice remains part of their signification (Peeren, 2014: 10)'.

I first applied Peeren's ideas to my research in an article, published in issue 16 of the journal *Laberintos*, titled 'José Ricardo Morales y la espectralidad: el caso del volumen *Fantasmagorías* de 1981' (2015, also included in this book). While preparing that particular essay, I realized how often Spanish Republican exiles referred to themselves as ghosts or specters. It was, in particular, acuter when they referred to their experiences back to the last years of General Franco's dictatorship and the democratic era in Spain. They coincide in explaining how they felt a lack of joint between their experience of Spain and the Spain of the seventies, eighties, and nineties. The cities reminded them of the cities they had left but were not the same anymore, the language reminded them of the language they knew, but it was different. In other words, cultural references, places, and ideas seemed out of place to them. Consequently, they felt also out of joint.

My final aim, in this book, is to study the Spanish literature in a singularity of disjoint rather than trying to fit it into the traditional canon. Neither do I want to consider exiles and disinherited artistic practices as members of an autonomous corpus aside Peninsular writings. The unicity of the exile resides in its spectral nature. In other words, the specificity of the Spanish Republican Exile requires the use of the notion of spectrality as a historiographic term to unveil modes of invisibility, cultural dialectics of presence/absence and empowerment.

This threshold opened with Kahn in 2004. Now it can be crossed. Therefore, this book is the result of more than fourteen years of work in progress. The reader will find essays written over the period 2004-2018. Some of these articles were tested in international conferences but have never been published in the present shape or they appeared in different less suitable contexts than the one offered here, and some others have not known publication yet or were not ever presented to public scrutiny.

As a reference to its structure, this volume follows a chronological division that I find useful for pedagogical purposes. I do not defend a linear evolution of ideas, but I do believe in circular and multidirectional processes of tension and hegemony —in the Gramscian's sense— which are articulated in chaotic superposition and partially ordered by the observation of a subject called Pablo Valdivia, with whom I share some tedious biographical details.

The central core of this book is made of different reflections on the particular field of the Spanish Republican Exile, but I have included some other texts, which contextualize and explain the spectral configuration of notions necessary to understand the specificity of such ideas in the Spanish literary tradition. Without exploring such concepts in other periods, writers and traditions, it would be far more complicated to proceed to a full understanding of spectral mechanisms for the configuration of the Spanish anomaly.

To conclude, I would like to bring to the reader's attention the opening words of *El amigo Manso* (1882) by Benito Pérez Galdós when the narrator assures that 'Yo no existo... Y por si algún desconfiado o terco o maliciosillo no creyese lo que tan llanamente digo, o exigiese algo de juramento para creerlo, juro y perjuro que no existo; y al mismo tiempo protesto contra toda inclinación o tendencia a suponerme investido de los inequívocos atributos de la existencia real'. In the previous quote, the character vindicates his right just to be 'fictional'. Indeed, as Manso, we all have the right to question the hegemonic discourses that, consciously and unconsciously, inscribe us with specific cultural practices. Spectres can see things from the inside and outside and be in two places at the same time likewise exiles whose double displaced condition leave them in an excellent position to give visibility to the inconvenient truths blinded by narratives of institutional power.

Works Cited

Aub, M. (1972). *El teatro español sacado a la luz de las tinieblas de nuestro tiempo.* Madrid: Triunfo.

Aznar Soler, M. (2002). 'La historia de las literaturas del exilio republicano español de 1939: problemas teóricos y metodológicos'. *Migraciones y Exilios*. 3. 9-22.

Derrida, J. (1995). *Espectros de Marx. El estado de la deuda, el trabajo del duelo y la nueva internacional.* Madrid: Trotta.

Gies, D. T. (2005). 'The Funes effect: making literary history'. *The Cambridge History of Spanish Literature*. 1-12. Cambridge: Cambridge University Press.

Kamen, H. (2007). *The Disinherited: Exile and the Making of Spanish Culture, 1492-1975.* London: Harper.

Machado, A. (2008). *Campos de Castilla.* Edited by Geoffrey Ribbans. Madrid: Cátedra.

Mainer, J. C. (2010). *Historia de la literatura española: 6. Modernidad y Nacionalismo (1900-1939).* Barcelona: Crítica.

Muñoz Molina, A. (1996). *Destierro y destiempo de Max Aub.* Madrid: Real Academia Española.

___. (2013). *Sefarad.* Edited by Pablo Valdivia. Madrid: Cátedra.

Okuefuna, D. (2008). *The Wonderful World of Albert Kahn: Colour Photographs from a Lost Age.* London: BBC Books.

Peeren, E. and Blanco, M. P. (2013). *The Spectralities Reader. Ghosts and Haunting in Contemporary Cultural Theory.* London: Bloomsbury.

___. (2014). *The Spectral Metaphor.* New York: Palgrave.

Pérez Galdós, B. (2006). *El amigo Manso.* Edited by Francisco Caudet. Madrid: Cátedra.

Preston, P. (2013). *The Spanish Holocaust: Inquisition and Extermination in Twentieth-Century Spain.* London: W.W. Norton & Company.

Valdivia, P. (2011). 'La recepción del proyecto artístico y ético de Lorca: hacia una reelaboración de la historia literaria española del siglo XX'. *Literatura y compromiso. Federico García Lorca y Miguel Hernández.* Madrid: Visor. 27-43.

___. (2015). 'José Ricardo Morales y la espectralidad: el caso del volumen *Fantasmagorías* de 1981'. *Laberintos.* 286-298.

2. Notes on a Haunted House: the Spanish Literary Canon

The Spanish 20th Century Literary Canon is, actually, a haunted house. Authors and works go in and out of the Spanish Canon depending on the political wind that blows or the academic fashions of each particular context or the misreadings and specific likes, dislikes and narrow-minded vision of the hegemonic cultural criticism. In parallel, the problem of what to do with a very uncomfortable relative, which is the Spanish Republican Exile, results in being an unfinished business.

In broad terms, there is a critical reluctance to abandon the scheme of the generations of writers in Spain —as it proved to be a useful tool for processes of auto-canonization and nationalist appropriation—. However, outside the Peninsula, the close-reading and diachronic/synchronic analysis of authors and works have been progressively replaced by an anxious compulsion to fit cultural products to theories rather than to enrich, with theoretical frameworks or without them, the readers' experience.

For instance, I remember (although I would instead prefer not to) a well-known university professor —whose name I will keep secret to save him from public shame— claiming that the reason why Cervantes never got recognition as a poet was the result of the hard competition he experienced with other authors such as Calderón de la Barca. The statement might sound nice to a non-informed audience, but it forgets the empirical fact that Calderón was barely 16 years old when Cervantes died and hardly could have competed against the author of *Don Quixote*.

I deliberately chose an example of the Early Modern Period to illustrate what usually becomes, even more, scarier in the field of Modern Spanish literature. The latter is a domain in which empirical accuracy is more and more unwelcome in the current academia.

In my view, academics need to return to the studies of diachronic and synchronic spaces that produced literary texts. Such new form of mingling Philosophy and Positivism, ideas and facts, should be complemented by the next four fundamental concepts which are, in my view, essential to for the study of the Republican Exile and contemporary Spanish Literature:

> **a) Spectrality:** The spectral metaphor can well summarise the exile condition. Exile writers suffer from the strangeness of being outlandish. They become specters invisible to the dominant national cultural discourses. In this regard, spectrality has a double meaning: on the one hand, it defines the condition of the exile and, on the other, it can also be understood as a historiographical notion that explains the presence/absence of exiles and the visibility/invisibility of their works.

> **b) Transnational:** Exiles transcend national boundaries. Their outlandish condition makes them be disinherited from any national discourse. However, the exclusion from the domestic realm does not place them in a supranational or international entity, but into the transnational sphere where the common denominator is the use of a shared language: Spanish. José Ricardo Morales is a good example. He arrived in Chile in 1940 and held both a Chilean and a Spanish passport. Morales had lived in Chile since then and visited Spain quite often during the '70s and '80s. Nevertheless, he was neither Chilean nor Spanish or, at least, he did not fit into the nationalistic construction, rooted in the authoritarian rules of Pinochet and Franco, of what

a Chilean or Spanish citizen should be. The blending of the two worlds, in this particular case, led to a hybrid transnational identity unique in its specificity.

c) Crisis: In its etymological definition, the medical term 'crisis' was used to name the highlight in which the patient could be cured or condemned to death. So, the notion of crisis, in the context of this book, would be used for defining unstable events in which radical changes and open paths for renewal took place. The exile is one of the most fundamental experiences of crisis as it disinherits individuals from everything familiar to them. After an event of a crisis, such as the Republican Exile of 1939, writers and intellectuals are forced to a new life in strange countries. This very moment of crisis is fundamental to understand the trauma of the exiles and how it becomes a departing point for their reconfiguration of their own new transnational identity(ies) and their cultural world of references.

d) Renewal: The crisis and trauma of the exile lead to an inevitable process of renewal. This renewal could be explicitly or implicitly presented in multiple modalities. There were exiles, such as Luis Cernuda, who lived their exile with nostalgia and in pain. Others, such as José Ricardo Morales, did not carried nostalgia. It led to a process of renewal in those countries in which the exiles developed their professional activities. To found and renew, was the aim and raison d'étre of these exiles who arrived in America not to obtain benefit but to contribute to developing democracy, education and culture. Exiles were dispossessed of everything except their experiences and expertise. Therefore, it is impossible to understand the Spanish

> Republican Exile without the transfusion of cultural references, structures, and initiatives to their new reality.

In 1946, the Argentinian Julio Cortázar wrote a fabulous short story titled 'Casa Tomada' ('House took over'), which was originally published in *Los Anales de Buenos Aires,* a literary magazine edited by Jorge Luis Borges and later included in the collection *Bestiario*. The story narrates how a brother and sister living together realize that their house is being taken over by unknown entities. The beginning of the realistic narrative style is progressively replaced by events that defy natural laws. Cortázar's haunted house concludes with the mystery of who or what has taken over. In my view, parallelism can be traced to the case of the Spanish Canon. Exiles are entities invisible to the inhabitants of the Spanish Canon but, as time passes by, and the house begins to need reforms and reparations not to fall apart, these entities become more and more visible. The exile playwright José Ricardo Morales provides a good example of this and explains how the identification of the notion of 'national identity' with 'national literature' is at the bottom of the problematic foundations of this haunted house.

In the late 19th Century, Philology was understood, along with another set of intellectual fields, as essential to the recovery of the most characteristic elements of the national or regional spirit. In the initial conception of Philology lies a substantial practical purpose: the location and analysis of those aspects of a nationality, which spiritually is embodied in art objects, to contribute to the cohesion of a pure and immutable identity (Cardwell, 1998). The result of this approach was the identification of Philology with the study of folklore and the pursuit of the *Volksgeist*.

Therefore, fin de siècle critics like Menéndez Pelayo (1856-1912) fully assumed that each national philology had an object of study a national language and a national corpus of texts, which represented the ideas and values which distinguished one national community from another better than any other art form.

However, this approach to literature produced a very problematic understanding of Spanish literature as for critics such as Menéndez Pelayo a text was, in its last form, nothing but the mirror of the Spanish national spirit.

Nevertheless, as we agree in the field of transnational studies, on the one hand the literary object escapes by definition any administrative attempt to be encapsulated. On the other hand, the imposition of sets of national values over texts always obliges to construct a national canon closed to any possible alterity that puts into question the uniqueness and the temporality of its essence (Guillén, 2005).

Consequently Philology, at the turn of the century in Spain, produced a pseudoscientific horizon, in debt to its times, which served to identify the idea of national literature with the notion of national identity. In other words, critics as Pelayo identified literature and nation; they created an essentialist intellectual discourse conceived to justify power interests and this process culminated in the configuration of a new theological discourse based on the ineffability of literaturness.

Theology is a form of speech that builds its object while using it as an authority to establish a prescribed dogma. A similar discursive operation was carried out in the philological field. In the process of identification between national identity and national literature, Philology created an object, the national canon, which was built from the basic premise that a text had more qualitative value if it reaffirmed the national beliefs and spirit. By following these ideas, the study of literature ceased to be interested in studying texts in their specificity and, subsequently, the humanistic analysis was replaced by a prescription of ideas, aesthetics, and books that contributed to consolidate the legitimacy of a particular political, economic, cultural and administrative model.

Despite Pelayo and his followers' attempt, History has proved that this nationalist way of understanding the literary object forged a terrible contradiction. On the contrary, reading is based on individual and emancipatory experience that no authoritarian discourse has ever managed to control. In other words, the basic principle of the exercise of reading is an open, cross-cultural and transnational experience in its nature (Albaladejo, 2011: 4). From the moment an author reads the work of another individual, a transferable relationship is created beyond any pretention to reduce meaning to a single possibility and, even less, to make it fit with national or regional narratives. The experience of reading always escapes dominant institutional discourses, as it is the only human act of full individual sovereignty. In this regard, neither the work of Cervantes can be understood without Erasmus. Nor the poetry of Quevedo without the Latin epigrammatic writing. Nor Juan Ramón Jiménez's late texts without studying English poetry. Nor Lorca's theatre without reading the Greek tragedies, and nor Muñoz Molina's fictional writing without Marcel Proust's prose. In short, any attempt of national ownership of a literary object always generates a tension between the individual reading experience and power-cultural nationalist discourses.

As the Spanish case demonstrates, the result —which we have synthetically exposed so far— has been the setting of Spanish literary historiography, based on late 19th Century determinist and nationalist ideas, heavily burdened with a very reductionist conception of the literary object. Such simplification has become extremist to the point of denying the principle of free reading texts and replacing the aesthetic and intellectual experience with a theological policy based on the faith in the national set of beliefs: the Spanish National Canon.

In this sense, for instance, turn of the century critics strategically read Cervantes. Firstly, they proceeded to identify national values in his works. Secondly, they theorized on how such national values were the product of the Spanish unique national spirit. Thirdly, they canonized authors and works to build up a theological narrative with literary apostles, bishops, and priests. The hierarchization of Spanish literature during the 20th Century has little to do with Bourdieu's 'literary field' notion or Zohar's 'polysystem', but with the copy and paste of Catholic mental structures and its application to literary labeling and artworks. Inevitably, such theologization of literature, especially acute during Francoist times, led to the inclusion/exclusion of texts and authors as they proportionally contributed to legitimizing power interests. According to Franco, he was the ruler of Spain by divine grace and the ultimate artist, as explained by Giménez Caballero in his famous *Arte y Estado* (1935), then the literary canon had to be, in nationalistic terms, the most significant sublimation of the Spanish spirituality.

The Francoism, as explained by Paul Preston (2012), defined its aim as the crusade against those who denied the Spanish essence. The participants of the coup d'état of 1936 did not see the Republicans as rivals but as a degeneration of the Spanish race. Therefore, it is not surprising that the first movie produced and written by Franco in 1942 was titled *Raza* (Race). In fact, the goal of the Francoism was to annihilate any form of alterity: from intellectual thinking to physical presence. Franco attempted, and succeeded to a substantial extent, to make a *tabula rasa* of Spain.

As a consequence, many writers and artists were assassinated just for the mere fact of representing the Other or a form of intellectual alterity. Or, if they were not killed or suffered any repression, they were forced to exile and, consequently, expelled from the theological, cultural narrative built up by the Francoism. One of the authors who has suffered from this national conception was the playwright and essayist José Ricardo Morales.

The legacy and work of José Ricardo Morales are some of the last witnesses of the intellectual life of the Second Spanish Republic (Aznar Soler, 2010). However, the critical reception of his dramatic writing and essays presented many difficulties for their full incorporation in the Spanish cultural system of the dictatorship and the democratic times (Monleón, 1969).

Morales was formed in the Spanish theatre scene of the thirties under the mastery of some notable figures such as Max Aub and the work performed in the theatre company of 'El Búho' in Valencia (Monléon, 1992). His artistic formation took place in an atmosphere of experimental inquiry. His first two works were represented in Valencia in those years until the outbreak of the Spanish Civil War and his enrolment in the Republican Army in which he fought until its final defeat.

Morales was one of the officials who covered the enormous wave of refugees who went to France to seek shelter and only found the barbed wire of the fields in which they were detained. José Ricardo himself, once already in France, was captured in 1939 and sent to the concentration camp of Saint-Cyprien (Valdivia Milla, 2010). He could not be released until his mother got a French businessman to declare himself responsible for the signing of the relevant documents on José Ricardo and his brother behalf.

José Ricardo's father, a prestigious chemist and pharmacist from Valencia, managed to obtain a work contract in Chile for the development of fertilizers and chemicals. A job like that was possible, among other reasons, because Chile and other Latin American countries were lacking in such highly skilled labour force. Then, José Ricardo and his family embarked the famous ship Winnipeg to Valparaíso. This was the first set of endless exiles that José Ricardo Morales and his work suffered until certain scholars such as Manuel Aznar Soler, José Monleón or Claudia Ortego, among others, began to gradually recover his theatre. In the words of Aznar Soler:

> José Ricardo Morales representa con absoluta propiedad el drama del dramaturgo exiliado español. Exiliado o —como él mismo prefiere— desterrado, desterrado por la fuerza como tantos republicanos vencidos: el drama del dramaturgo desterrado, sin tierra y sin público. Porque desde que el 18 de julio de 1936 una sublevación militar fascista, encabezada por el general Franco, se alzase contra la legalidad democrática republicana y desencadenase así nuestra guerra civil, el desenlace de esa tragedia para cualquier español 'leal' sólo podía ser, por utilizar palabras del propio autor, uno entre tres: el de 'enterrado' (Federico García Lorca); el de 'aterrado', esa España 'cautiva y desarmada' que fue condenada a un *insilio* hecho de miedo, silencio y hambre (los prisioneros Buero Vallejo o Miguel Hernández, muerto éste último en una cárcel franquista); o el de 'desterrado' (Alberti, Aub y tantos más, cuya primera experiencia fueron los campos de concentración), esa *España peregrina* de que hablara José Bergamín, la España *del éxodo y del llanto* que, según León Felipe, se llevó consigo al exilio la voz y la canción, la palabra poética del pueblo español (Aznar Soler, 2010: 9-10).

Not without reason, Aznar Soler defined Morales as an 'exiled playwright, landless and publicless'. In this sense, although José Ricardo suffered the same tragic events that many other Republicans, Morales' position regarding the issue of the exile offers features that distinguish himself from the narrative commonly created by most Spanish exiles as he declares to not suffer from any nostalgia.

It is important to note that, when Morales left Spain he still was very young. Morales was born in 1915, and when he reached the Chilean coast, he had a lifetime ahead. In the new country, he resumed his university studies, consolidated a vigorous academic career as a professor of Theory and History of Art and Architecture at the University of Chile and the Catholic University of Chile. Also, he was appointed to the Academy of Language in Chile, while he developed his artistic and intellectual career as a playwright, essayist, and painter (Diago, 2005).

Therefore, we are not facing a young Republican who aims to 'hacer las Américas' (a common expression used for describing those Spaniards who saw America as a source to obtain wealth) but to contribute 'hacer que América se hiciera' (to empower America), as he has stated on many occasions (Morales, 2000). Thus, Morales never tried to create a portrait of himself as an 'official exile' or a 'professional exile' (at it was the notorious case of Rafael Alberti). Conversely, Morales focussed his energy on making possible the transfusion of structures and cultural projects that previously existed in the pre-Spanish Civil War context.

José Ricardo Morales understood his exile, rather than the misfortune of a particularly tragic situation, as a condition which has recurrently occurred in Spanish history (Monleón, 1973). Likewise, also Claudio Guillén exposed this idea, forty years later after Morales' exile, in his study *El Sol de los exiliados* (1995). Indeed, José Ricardo, whose visionary cultural practice is a crucial feature in his writings, saw his exile as a part of a universal condition. Morales particular manner of understanding his exile condition allowed him to develop a transnational dramatic language based on the notion of dispossession (Morales, 2000).

In this regard, Morales argues that the word 'exile' conveys a sense of dispossession which the Spanish term 'exile' lacks. The articulation of the concept of 'exile' is one of the leading elements in his dramatic texts. For Morales, the world is textual, and our ability to interact with it and the other lies in the discursive configuration of language as an object which is constantly updated, twisted and modified. This fact has led critics to a misunderstanding of his works as they labeled them under the frame of 'absurd theatre'. However, Morales plays were written a long time before Beckett's or Ionesco's works. Morales' dramas moved in the contradictions created by the 'absurdity of the world' and the 'dispossession' that humans suffer in modern times. This very idea is one of the cornerstones of its entire production since his earliest works (Morales, 1992).

The source of Morales' notion of exile has roots in the philosophical thought of Ortega y Gasset. Exile is, in Morales' view, the result of the dehumanization of the individual. Therefore, Morales conceives his 'exile' in connection to a universal narrative of dispossession, regardless of time frames, geographical spaces or language barriers (Muñoz Cáliz, 2010). As Morales explained in his own words:

> Es cosa sabida que 'desterrar', de acuerdo con el diccionario, supone 'echar a uno por justicia de un territorio o lugar'. De donde cabe deducir que la justicia, en cuanto concierne al medio millón de españoles que fuimos arrojados a ninguna parte por las huestes de Franco, Hitler y Mussolini, la establecieron quienes lograron imponer su fuerza sobre un régimen libre, la República, en un acto que sólo tiene el precedente cuantitativo de los millares de judíos y moriscos expulsados, contra justicia, promesas y ley, tanto por los Reyes Católicos cuanto por los Austrias. No obstante, según se deduce de ésta y otras publicaciones análogas, muchos hicieron suyo nuestro destino, que afectó, quiérese o no, a España entera. Porque difícilmente puede resarcirse un país de pérdida tan severa como la experimentada entonces por el nuestro en su capital mayor: me refiero a sus cabezas, impedidas de actuar y producir allí donde hubieran deseado, en su tierra. De tal modo ese pretendido acto de justicia ocasionó

> *la más considerable malversación de talentos sufrida últimamente por España*, puesto que fueron obligados a trabajar fuera de sí y de lo suyo, corroborándose con ello que la palabra 'desterrar', debido a su considerable extensión y a la frecuencia de su uso, no en vano es una de las más genuinas que haya forjado el castellano (Morales, 2010: 37).

For these reasons, the universal nature of the thought and work of José Ricardo Morales has sharply clashed with the Spanish national canon. Francoism and late official interventions in the canon invisibilized Morales' intellectual production (Novella, 1999). This exclusion produced a paradox. Morales has been regarded a Spanish writer in Chile for the Chilean national canon —among other reasons because the language of his works does not follow local dialects—; and, in Spain, his physical absence has been translated into oblivion or to the wrong assumption that Morales is a Latin-American artist.

Thus, it does not surprise us the little attention brought to Morales' works as they are fundamentally transnational. In this regard, Morales represents an uncomfortable and dangerous position for any power nationalistic based narratives, which operate under the goal of legitimizing political programmes (Mengual, 1992). Such confrontation especially occurs in Morales case because his writings present a form of alterity which results in the questioning of any essentialist discourse. Morales lives in Chile, publishes in Spain and finds his readers and public among the Spanish speaking world republic of letters. Therefore, Morales occupies an intellectual space where the 'rules' of the nationalistic 'physics' do not apply and fail to explain works and authors. Here, the transnational becomes a specter which undermines the principles of the Spanish National Canon.

Hence, for Morales, the written word has great importance as he believes that each term carries a certain baggage of meaning and power, a symbolic cultural capital, which art must use to empower the individual and to avoid any nationalist manipulation or appropriation (Castedo Ellerman, 1992). It this sense, for Morales to understand the journey suffered by words throughout history equally means apprehending the processes of how our thinking is articulated.

Morales believes that the playwright has to assume the role of a sort of 'Socratic mosquito' which should pinch and raise self-awareness among the spectators. The procedure he uses to fulfill that function is systematically dismantling, through irony, any possibility that the language can present an essentialist shape. Therefore, Morales plays with double meanings or paradoxes to challenge, through meta-textual interventions, a fixed and transcendental ideological space (Ortego Sanmartin, 2002).

In this regard, José Ricardo Morales developed what he termed as 'theatre of uncertainty' (Morales, 2000). If we pay attention to all of his works, the issues we find are utterly contemporary but at the same time universal because these issues are not rooted in any temporal or geographical localism: human objectification, the nuclear danger, the tension between ethics and technological development, technology as displaced theology, isolation, corruption, State repression, terrorism, the development of the consumer society.

Due to his exile condition, José Ricardo soon realized that any articulation of intellectual thought is always structured in a double diachronic and synchronic process, which also carries the existence of a double that denies and reaffirms it at the same time. Ambiguities, contradictions, which are a constant in the works of our author, are discursive strategies to provoke a principle of uncertainty in the viewer, of not knowing whether this is said seriously or half-serious and half-joking, that automatically results in an effect of estrangement which necessarily requires reflection and critical exercise.

Likewise, Miguel de Unamuno and Antonio Machado explained, in the early twentieth century, there was no distinction between literature and philosophy. For Machado intellectual thought was based on a poetic principle. For him, the moment in which through a mere convention we assign meaning to a signifier, we are running a poetic operation. Antonio Machado understands that thought is articulated through a set of discursive strategies and that, therefore, poetry presents an opportunity to delve into the nature of what Kant called the conflict of transcendental ideas. For its part Unamuno, he also started from a similar active departing principle. His novels and poetry constitute the narrative unfolding of a set of paradoxes. These paradoxes have a direct relationship with its present social time and also bring us to reflect on universal problems of the human condition. As Morales acutely noted:

> El teatro puede considerarse como el arte que revela a la persona en el acto de asumir o resolver las situaciones conflictivas que le afectan. Estimado de tal modo, dicho arte corresponde por entero a la condición del hombre, ya que 'el sí mismo' de éste requiere que cada cual, para poder conocerse, haya de situarse ante sí, desdoblándose, hecho un esquizoide cuerdo. Hasta el punto que el modelo de semejante aptitud humana lo atribuyó el pensamiento aristotélico a la divinidad, entendida como un ser cuya labor primordial consiste en reflexionar eternamente sobre él. Nada menos (Morales, 2010: 37).

This same horizon is beating under José Ricardo Morales' plays. His theatre never departs from a situation but does it from a philosophical conflict, a tension at the ideological level. José Ricardo Morales can overcome the mere idealism to take it to a higher level of transgression and subversion. In other words, from my perspective, with his plays, José Ricardo Morales opens a whole new paradigm about a different way of understanding the theatrical performance. Such manner of addressing ideological conflicts unveils the intellectual power structures which configure the public sphere:

> Por otra parte, con mis obras iniciales también abordé el problema del hacer propio del drama, en el entendido de que aunque éste supone acción, los actos que la componen no han de ser indiferentes ni han de resultar inocuos a quienes los efectúan, pues tienen que ocasionar consecuencias conflictivas, opuestas en muchos casos a los propósitos que los originaron. De tal modo, esta reversión posible entre nuestras intenciones, los actos que motivaron y su resultado adverso trae consigo la inseguridad del personaje y la del espectador. Por ello, la inconsecuencia posible entre nuestros propósitos y sus impredecibles resultados me hizo calificar las obras en que la expuse como 'un teatro de la incertidumbre' (Morales, 2010: 38-39).

Here is one of the significant findings, in my opinion, of José Ricardo Morales' literary discourse: he manages to dive into the most complex and dark areas of our societies, and to both dismantle the intellectual and ideological mechanisms that sustain the practices of power on which our civilization is pillared.

To shed light on my analysis, I will illustrate with an example what has been presented. In Morales' play *La corrupción al alcance de todos* (1996) one of the leading characters is a mummy. This subtle effect is masterful. Firstly, the audience sees a mummy, and they might find a talking mummy nonsensical. Then they discover parallels with the world they know, and eventually they end up reflecting, albeit with a smile and perhaps almost in an unconscious way, about the relationship between power and corruption: Can there be anyone more corrupt than a mummy? In this play, the answer is yes: a policeman looking for a bribe and a museum curator who does not mind getting rid of an art-work piece if she gets some benefit with the transaction.

Morales plays present a demystifying principle. He will name this 'españoladas' (Godoy Gallardo, 2001). Morales deconstructs the principles of the national. According to Morales and contrary to what many may think, Herder's theories on a natural community, *Volksgeist*, or the Schlegel ideas are, unfortunately, the intellectual foundations for the representation of nation-building. Herder argued that each natural community corresponded to a territory with a certain set of traditions and customs in which the spirit of the community was reflected. This same principle has been followed in the modern nation-building of each country or region. In the case of Spain, as José Ricardo Morales explains it, a particular building has been carried out around certain myths such as 'Don Juan' (Gómez, 1992).

José Ricardo presented in his 'españoladas' (in works like *Ardor con ardor se apaga* or *El torero por las astas*) a sort of deconstruction *avant la lettre*. Morales attempts to unveil how the building up of a national imaginary is performed from the inside and outside a given community. Both internal and external 'españoladas' reaffirm stereotypes. From their blind eyes, stereotypes persist in the collective perception imposed, constructed and exported at the same time.

Morales' public soon notes 'españoladas' notes that such stereotypes respond to an interest-driven ideological construction. Thus, Morales demystifies nationalistic discourses using irony. In the course of this intellectual operation, the audience is forced to exercise critical thinking (Ortego Sanmartin, 1992).

José Ricardo Morales' theatre has a clear transgressive element employing the word that reveals the ideological principles that serve as justification for any totalitarianism or manipulation. His humor is deeply engaged with the writings of Ramón Gómez de la Serna (1888-1963) and theatrical concepts enunciated by Valle-Inclán in *Ligazón* (1926) in which bitter moments of drama and intense poetic emotion come together.

Examples of this are to be found in his works grouped under the name of *Teatro en Libertad* (1984) and in his 'dramatic announcements' and 'phantasmagorias'. Among these various plays, there is one especially relevant title *Oficio de tinieblas* (1966), one of José Ricardo's masterpieces, which was represented in Spain for the first time in 2014 and could be described, from our perspective, as one of the works most disturbingly written in Spanish. In a completely dark room, the word takes on its most fundamental sense: the voices of the actors give life to the drama of living with those wounds which landmark the emotional geography of our memories.

On several occasions, José Ricardo Morales has said that humankind is always in exile. Not without reason, his works might well occupy one of the leading places of the Hispanic transnational culture of the 20th and 21st Century. José Ricardo Morales has warned us, in his dramas and essays, about the dangers of considering that technological progression entails a similar linear progressive development in human thought and rights. Conversely, History has shown us that such relationship is just an illusion. Intellectual and aesthetic ideas never advance following a linear pattern, but they suffer all kinds of alterations. The teleological principle is nothing but a fallacy. In this regard, Morales makes a clear statement in his drama *Orfeo y el desodorante* and *Prohibida la reproducción*, just to mention few examples that reassure my views, based on the premise that exile is both a transnational and individual experience:

> La impresión primera que se tiene en el destierro es, forzosamente, la del extrañamiento. Se vive en un mundo que, por ser ajeno, nos obliga a 'asistir' a él como espectadores, con plena lucidez, en absoluta situación de desprendimiento (Morales, 2010: 15).

Morales suffered an endless succession of exiles —political exile, censorship and nationalistic stereotypes— that have marked his life and work from the 1939 Republican exile to banishment from the stage because of the censorship or nationalistic discourses in Chile and Spain. Therefore, I conclude that his continued exile from the Spanish traditional literary canon and his spectrality was caused by the sum of political and cultural power interests that had nothing to do with the quality of his works.

Finally, as José Ricardo Morales maintains, not without subtle irony, 'the precursors are always late'. I do believe that it is time to expose the specter and, therefore, to study Morales' intellectual and artistic legacy to a new Spanish culture which pays tribute and critical attention to its transnational nature (Ferrater Mora, 1967). I do hope that the considerations presented in these pages will contribute to bring more interest to the work of José Ricardo Morales and his banishment from the scope of the Spanish culture, that has overpassed a century, will end with a warm embrace of recognition and attention shown by new readers, by new scholars who will continue to discover his legacy and by new courageous scene professionals who dare to bring Morales' place to the stage. I have demonstrated, by taking Morales' case to the front, that the Spanish Literary Canon is a haunted house. It is about time to confront our specters and provide visibility to those who were traditionally marginalized by nationalist cultural narratives. Follow me through this haunted home and the next pages journey.

Works Cited

Ahumada, H. (2000). 'José Ricardo Morales a la intemperie'. *Signos* XXIII. 48.

Albaladejo, T. (2011). 'Literaturas europeas e interculturalidad'. *Paseos literarios por la Europa intercultural*. Madrid: Calambur. 1-8.

Aznar Soler, M. (2010). *Obras completas* by José Ricardo Morales. Valencia: Fundación Alfons Magnanim.

Cardwell, R. (1998). 'Antonio Machado and the Search for the Soul of Spain: A Genealogy'. *Anales de la literatura contemporánea*. Vol. 23. 1/2. 51-79.

Castedo-Ellerman, E. (1992). 'Un dramaturgo que valora la palabra: José Ricardo Morales'. *Anthropos* 133 (June), 47-49.

Diago, N. (2005). 'El dramaturgo en su exilio'. *El embustero en su enredo*. Valencia: Universitat de València. 9-14.

Ferrater Mora, J. (1967). 'Sobre la fama'. *Obras selectas*. Madrid: Revista de Occidente. II; reproduced in Morales, José Ricardo. *Teatro*. Madrid: Taurus, El Mirlo Blanco. 45-51.

Godoy Gallardo, E. (2001). 'Teoría y práctica de las *Españoladas* en el teatro de José Ricardo Morales'. *Revista Signos*- XXXIV. 49-50; 21-33.

Gómez González, J. (1992). 'Españoladas, de José Ricardo Morales'. *Anthropos*, 133 (June). 77-80.

Guillén, C. (1995). *El sol de los desterrados*. Barcelona: Sirmio.

___. (2005). *Entre lo uno y lo diverso*. Barcelona: Tusquets.

Mengual Catalá, J. (1992). 'El lenguaje como tema en *Teatro en libertad*', *Anthropos*, 133 (June). 72-77.

Monleón, J. (1969). 'Morales, un español en la inmensa ninguna parte'. In Morales, José Ricardo. *Teatro*. Madrid: Taurus. Colección El Mirlo Blanco. 9-28.

___. (1973). 'Con José Ricardo Morales, peregrino en su patria y autor de ninguna parte', *Triunfo*, 563 (July). 34-36.

___. (1992). 'Max Aub y José Ricardo Morales, dos dramaturgos de la España marginal', *Anthropos*, 133 (June). 60-62.

Morales, J. R. (2000). *Ensayos en suma*. Madrid: Editorial Biblioteca Nueva.

___. (1992). *Mímesis Dramática*. Santiago de Chile-Madrid: Editorial Universitaria y Primer Acto.

Muñoz Cáliz, B. (2010). *Censura y teatro del exilio*. Murcia: Universidad de Murcia.

Novella, N. (1999). 'Simbiosis entre exilio y absurdidad en la dramaturgia de José Ricardo Morales'. *60 años después. Os escritores do exilio republicano*. Sant Cugat del Vallès: Associació d'Idees GEXEL. Colección Sinaia. 303-330.

Ortego Sanmartín, C. (1992). 'Reflexiones sobre *Españoladas*'. *Anthropos*. 133 (June). 80-86.

___. (2002). 'José Ricardo Morales: un escritor en el "aparte" del destierro'. *Teatro ausente*. Sada: Ediciós do Castro, Biblioteca del Exilio. 7-67.

Valdivia Milla, B. y Galeote, M. (2010). 'Vivir como extranjero: a propósito de José Ricardo Morales Malva'. Granada: Junta de Andalucía, Biblioteca Virtual de Andalucía.

3. Juan del Encina's room: the specter of a new author and reader

As earlier explained, I believe we cannot assess the contemporary transnational Spanish literature without conceptualizing before a particular framework of ideas and contradictions. In my opinion, what we understand nowadays as 'literature' in the Spanish tradition is the result of two key historical moments: one took place at the end of the 15th Century epitomized by the case of Juan del Encina; and, the other, brings us to the end of the 16th Century as we will explore in the next chapter about Cervantes. Both authors were marginalized and invisibilized to an important extent of their lives. They inhabited the margins. Consequently, they wrote and conceived literature from/inside the margins of the hegemonic cultural powers of their times. In other words, they were specters, and still they are to an important extent as both, Encina and Cervantes, have gained critical attention but never as marginal writers but through the lenses of distorted and mythical fictions created to fulfill the political goals of the Menéndez Pelayo's nationalist school, which had high acceptance in the Francoist academia.

Conversely, here, Juan del Encina interests me as somebody who had a marginal position in the Spanish letters. Juan del Encina (1468-1529) is traditionally considered as a poet, musician, and playwright of the pre-Reinassance. In 1496, he published his *Cancionero*, a collection of dramatic and lyrical poems. Then Encina applied for the cantor post at Salamanca Cathedral, but the position was divided among three candidates, including his rival Lucas Fernández. After this, he left for Italy where he relocated in Rome until he was appointed, in 1508, Archdiaconate of Málaga Cathedral by Julius II.

Additionally, academic traditional literary criticism presents an essential problem carried out during decades by many scholars: the compulsive need for encapsulating authors in fixed periods or labeling as pre- or post- when they do not have a bright idea of what to do with them. Following such ideas, an author cannot be studied out of his assignment to fixed characteristics. Furthermore, there is a general assumption to believe that the closer an author is to us, in historical terms, the more modern his/her literary discourse is.

Nevertheless, such mental scheme is dismantled when we have to face the writings of authors where the chronological divide is much more unclear. For these authors, traditional criticism has created the tricky territory of the 'transitional'. If it is too obvious that the texts produced by an author do not belong to the critical-chronological scheme accepted then, instead of assessing his writings by their qualities and circumstances, academics tend to invent non-defined spaces for *ad hoc* 'problematic writers'.

By this procedure, the author —as Encina's case— has become a singularity for the scholar who does not question his/her mental scheme. A critic with this set of ideas does not contemplate the fact that the author does not write about fulfilling *a posteriori* academic category. In other words, it is my firm belief that we have compulsively replaced what the texts say in each given historical conjuncture by what our traditional scheme of literary notions tells us they must be.

It applies to Juan del Encina's case in my view. Some critics have described his works as belonging to the Middle Age, others as part of the Renaissance production and, finally, few who argued that he is what we can define as a 'transitional' or 'pre-Renaissance' author.

I think the three definitions are wrong by the preconceived notions they hold. In this regard, I will propose a new assessment of Encina's *Arte de poesía castellana* (1496) in the next pages, and I will leave aside the traditional considerations to determine if the text entirely belongs to a period or other, or just respond to the characteristics of a so-called transitional territory.

Arte de poesía castellana represents, to my view, a strange spectral singularity. Scholars have traditionally encountered this text from the field of the history of the ideas. They paid special attention to what the *Arte* apparently reproduces on rhetoric, poetic meter and style from the perspective of its relationship with the medieval literary tradition. Fixing the sources and influences of Encina's approach to verse composition has been a common pattern when approaching this work. On this sense, I think it is relevant to remind Julian Weiss' comments stated in his article 'Tiempo y materia en la poética de Juan del Encina':

> Hasta la fecha, se ha analizado el *Arte* desde la perspectiva de la historia de las ideas. Una consecuencia positiva y fundamental de dicho procedimiento es que se ha dilucidado el significado y las fuentes de los conceptos teóricos de la obra —con una excepción importantísima, como se indicará en su momento. Por otra parte, el método entraña la búsqueda de un 'sistema coherente' de ideas, que en nuestro caso pertenecen a las del humanismo renacentista. Por tanto, el sentido histórico de la obra se ha evaluado en la medida en que se conforma a, y reproduce, los parámetros de este 'sistema' cultural (Weiss, 1999: 243).

Weiss' words support my earlier remarks. I consider his assertions especially outstanding as he underlines the need for comprehending *Arte de poesía castellana* in its specificity and not from the adequacy of specific academic preconceived patterns.

Why is *Arte de poesía castellana* so different? What makes it special? In my opinion, this text written by Encina is essential to understand the forging of a new notion of subjectivity —spectral in its essence—, which will be the base of our 'take-for-granted' idea on what is to write poetry now, what is an author and what kind of public could potentially be addressed.

We must come back to other Encina's work to start the analysis. In his translation to Virgil's *Églogas*, he will manifest in the prologue that he found himself forced to 'impropiar las palabras, y acrecentar o menguar según hiziere a mi caso'. Indeed, it is a justification but in addition to it that represents the articulation of a text in order to fulfill a new necessity. As Weiss explained in his essay:

> Además, no sólo se pierde algo del sentido original, sino que parte del original se escapa de la aplicación alegórica a los Reyes Católicos. Más que una distorsión, Encina presenta esto como un proceso creativo, cuyos parámetros son determinados por la necesidad de conciliar textos y órdenes sociales del pasado y del presente. En este proceso dialéctico, el poeta toma conciencia de 'mi caso', y de sí mismo como *sujeto* dentro de un orden social y temporal (Weiss, 1999: 250).

Complementary to Weiss reading, I find suggestive Jeremy Lawrance's analysis on the *Églogas*. Lawrance in an acute article evaluates the link between Encina's translation and the realm of the Catholic Kings' court:

> The court is seen not only as the fount of patronage and cynosure of civilized fashion and gallantry but also as an epicenter of power where the mere sight of the royal presence operates like some heavenly *visión amorosa* (Lawrance, 2004: 25-26).

And precisely is to this direction to where I want to drive my meditation about Encina's *Arte de poesía castellana*. In other words, what Weiss and Lawrance are mentioning is the fact that Encina places us before a process for the re-configuration of the public sphere.

The union of kingdoms performed by the marriage of Fernando and Isabel and subsequent annexations of other territories brought essential and radical changes. One of the implications will be to develop a new bureaucratic and legal system to govern the vast areas. At the end of the 15th Century Encina is still far from the following implementation of an extensive bureaucratic apparatus like the ones of the reigns of Carlos V and Felipe II, but the printed letter, the paper, will already acquire in time of the Catholic Kings a fundamental dimension in the society.

At the end of the 15th Century, in a moment of intense changes, new opportunities were available at the court for those who were able to gain the favor of the power. We are at the start of considering literature as a vehicle to promote individual status.

If in the dominant medieval ideology the relation between the 'trovador' and the power was a pact of vassalage, under the Catholic Kings' times, instead, it is introduced a contract of servitude based on the social conventions of the merit and the unconditional love of the servant towards his masters.

This change is the result of a new consideration on what the public sphere is. The reason for this new understanding is deeply attached to the creation of a nation-state where the mercantile exchange has superseded the feudal model of the exploitation of the resources. A clear example of this is the fact that a Royal apparatus will actively control the exploitation of the Western Indies, 'La Casa de Contratación', which will result on a new level of intermediaries, distributors and financial capitals that, at the same time, will re-draw the map of the relationships among the different members and society actors.

Castile, we might not forget this, was under a policy of expansionism, with the conquest of the Kingdom of Granada and the Western Indies, and in a context of nationalistic reaffirmation. Such reaffirmation drove into supremacy, within the Mediterranean context, from the moment that Castile made Western Indies' conquest possible and established an exclusive contract of natural resources exploitation.

Subsequently to the political and economic authoritarian programme carried out by the Catholic Kings, it was developed in parallel a cultural and linguistic political agenda too. Nebrija with his *Arte romance* filled the gap of providing the Crown with a linguistic treaty, which would fix the Castilian for its use. Accordingly, to this path, Encina was conscious of the necessity for creating a new figure sustained on the written *auctoritas*. Encina desired to consolidate his position not only in the 'present' of the court but the 'tomorrow' of the new literary tradition in Castilian language. Nebrija and Encina's strategic turn to the 'future' implied the development of a very modern idea of what authorship and readership had to be.

In relation to the notion of authorship, it is obvious the step given by Encina from 'trovador' to 'poeta' as articulated in *Arte de poesía castellana*:

> Y confiando en la virtud de vuestra real magestad, atrevíme a dedicar esta obra a su ecelente ingenio, donde ya florecen los remos de la sabiduría, para si fuere servido, estando desocupado de sus arduos negocios, exercitarse en cosas poéticas y trobadas en nuestro castellano estilo, porque lo que ya su bivo juyzio por natural razón conoce, lo pueda ver puesto en arte, según lo que mi flaco saber alcança; no porque crea que los poetas y trobadores se ayan de regir por ella, siendo yo el menor dellos, mas por no ser ingrato a esta facultad si algún nombre me ha dado, o si merezco tener siquiera el más baxo lugar entre los **poetas** de nuestra nación (Encina, 1978: 7-8).

I find very interesting the previous fragment as Encina provides the reader with his view about his role. Encina defines himself as a 'poeta' and makes a difference between a 'poeta' and 'trovador'. But 'poeta', we cannot forget it, was a term used to denominate those who wrote verse in Latin and not in vernacular. In addition to this, Encina's *Arte de poesía castellana* is the heading of what he calls a 'copilación' of his works. It is, at least, remarkable as authors of works in verses used to spread their writings in manuscripts that, maybe later on if lucky, received the privilege to be published and be commentated. The case of an author, who publishes his writings and comments them with a theoretical body of appraisals, is genuinely innovative at this time. Encina will add in his *Arte*:

> Según es común uso de hablar en nuestra lengua, al trobador llaman poeta y al poeta trobador, ora guarde la ley de los metros ora no; mas a mí me parece que quanta diferencia ay entre músico y cantor, entre geómetra y pedrero, tanta deve aver entre poeta y trobador (Encina, 1978: 17-18).

So Encina, 'un poeta', prints his works in a context where none published his works; and books were precious commodities. It is in line with a more complicated process that took place in the 15th Century, which implies the delocalization of the centres of knowledge from the monasteries and the clerical surrounding to the world of the courts. I agree with the clarifying explanation of such phenomena in the words of Ottavio di Camillo:

> A medida que reyes y nobles se fueron interesando en actividades intelectuales, tradicionalmente limitadas a la clerecía, los centros de investigación se fueron desplazando, de las escuelas y monasterios, a la atmósfera

> mundana de las cortes y a las bibliotecas señoriales. Pero los libros suponían una considerable inversión de dinero y muy pocos podían permitirse tal lujo; los nobles que podían, o carecían de instrucción, o estaban demasiado ocupados con la administración de sus propios asuntos para poder dedicarse de lleno a la cultura. Lo que algunos hicieron fue comprar libros y rodearse de personas instruidas, capaces de traducir y transcribir textos y conversar con sus protectores sobre literatura o cuestiones filosóficas (1976: 113).

Indeed a new kind of 'ocio' is arising in the courts and figures like Encina are meant to be the main characters of that picture. Encina knew it. It is why I insist again. Behind Encina's purpose, there is a nationalistic reason, but the actual engine of his choice and the impulse to define a new figure as 'el poeta' is mainly an issue of sociological and cultural dimension.

So far, we have outlined a new notion of authorship with Encina. If the 'trovador' was a mere entertainment at the same level than other courtesan activities, now 'el poeta' will occupy a didactic place and the position of provider of knowledge and intellectual *auctoritas*. Complementary to the new realm I am describing, Ottavio di Camillo wrote some fortunate thoughts on the issue:

> Esta es la moralidad dominante en la sociedad vivida por los personajes de *La Celestina*. Como Maravall ha apuntado convincentemente, es una sociedad materialista en la que prospera un nuevo tipo humano, 'el ocioso honorable'. Para este tiempo, 'la ley del ocio ostensible' junto con 'la ley del gasto ostensible' se han vuelto 'los dos fundamentos' de la posición social para 'la nueva clase de adinerados', a la que pertenecen Calisto y Melibea. Debemos añadir que el 'ocio'

> no es definido como aquel intervalo entre acciones, según fue caracterizado dos generaciones antes, ni tampoco es tiempo libre dedicado a actividades intelectuales. Habiendo sido el valor moral de la actividad práctica reemplazado por el social de la inactividad ostensible, el 'ocio' ha venido a parar en la nueva 'ocupación' (Camillo, 1976: 113).

I consider that a new idea of the authorship role emerged in connection to the previous activities is quite clear. On this regard, there is another question we should address. If a new authorship notion arose was because there was a re-definition of the idea of readership too.

Indeed, *Arte de poesía castellana* presents various ways to be approached, and one is its importance as an engine to forge a new 'reader'. As Weiss did in his informative and sensible book entitled as *The poet's art*, the tradition of poetics in Castilian language has its roots in the texts of Enrique Villena's *Arte de trobar* and *Carta-Prohemio* by Marqués de Santillana mainly. However, there are two big differences between Encina's *Arte de poesía castellana*. Neither, Santillana or Villena, have a 'historical' conception of his poetics. Villena and Santillana's texts have more of an authorized body of recommendations than an assumption of what means to write verse in Castilian, for what purpose and under what conditions.

Many critics have argued that Encina's *Arte de poesía castellana* is primarily medieval in its considerations on the poetic meter. It is true that he does not add a revolutionary or new, in any sense, appraisal on that respect. However, I am afraid that was not Encina's purpose at all developing a further point about this. If we are looking for a treaty on poetic meter, we will not find that in the straight sense. We will be wrong if we neglect following Encina's assertion:

> En lo primero amonestamos a los que carecen de ingenio y son más aptos para otros estudios y exercicios, que no gasten su tiempo en vano leyendo nuestros precetos, podiéndolo emplear en otra cosa que les sea más natural, y tomen por sí aquel dicho de Quintiliano, en el primero de sus *Instituciones*, que ninguna cosa aprovechan las artes y precetos, adonde fallece natura, que a quien ingenio falta, no le aprovecha más esta arte que precetos de agricultura a tierras estériles (1978: 18-19).

The election of the word 'ingenio' above 'preceto' it is crucial. 'Ingenio' is a human quality that applies only to the chosen ones. The theological 'genio' is replaced by the secular 'ingenio' and thanks to the personal 'ingenio' of the individual is how the virtue, as an absolute value, can be reached. My point is that the technical terms or the constant allusion to medieval *auctoritas* as Cicero or Quintilian are rather 'excuses' for something else. In other words, Encina is not worried about the 'cognitio terminorum', he considers that is just necessary to establish certain rules as the mold that will fix the quality of poetry. Encina concern is much more profound; he cares about the 'cognitio rerum' and the promotion of the 'poet' figure as an indispensable advisor to the rule of Power.

Encina knows, at the moment he decides to publish his works and to create *Arte de poesía castellana*, that he is building History but also he is attempting to make himself visible as a poet: the spectre is, in this sense, trying to become present. Is that compelling reason for the existence of past, present and future in a very similar way to how we understand it now, what is making the difference. For the so-called medieval poets as Santillana, Mena o Villena, there is nothing such a historical past as a systemic process. They consider there is just an extension of their present. Nonetheless, Encina, well aware of his today as a specter, understands the need for the noble duty of attaching his 'praxis' to not series of *auctoritas* but to a tradition of knowledge and wisdom. Weiss attempt to explain this issue on Encina's *Arte de poesía castellana* was the following:

> Al igual que Baena y Santillana, Encina sitúa la poesía dentro de una red de prácticas culturales. Estos escritores, sin embargo, lo hacían para demostrar que la poesía era el pasatiempo más noble del cortesano (en el caso de Baena); o para demostrar que era connatural al hombre —vivir es hacer versos (en el caso de Santillana). Encina, en cambio, pone más énfasis en la poesía como una praxis social, que es un proceso dinámico y transformativo, puesto que en el paso del dominio de la necesidad al dominio de la gala, lo que inicialmente es chocante se acepta como 'normal', 'natural', o incluso objeto de ostentación artística (Weiss, 1999: 248).

Agrceing with the complementary analysis performed by Weiss and in connection to my views, I could add that such transformative dimension of the poetic-social praxis is due to the existence, in a dialectic interaction, of a new kind of reader too.

Despite the *Arte de poesía castellana* is dedicated to the prince Don Juan, the scope of the text is broader. The courts were filled not only by the members of the royalty but with businessmen and other court actors looking for prospective opportunities in this micro-political context. Encina makes this point clear at the beginning of his *Arte de poesía castellana*:

> Cuán ligero y penetrable fuesse el ingenio de los antiguos y cuán enemigos de la ociosidad, muy esclarecido príncipe, notorio es a vuestra alteza, como cuenta Cicerón de Africano el mayor, que dezía nunca estar

> menos ocioso que quando estava ocioso ni menos solo que quando solo, dando a entender que nunca holgava su juyzio (Encina, 1978: 6).

And he continues on the reaffirmation of this new subjectivity:

> Y según sentencia de aquel Catón censorino, no solamente son obligados los hombres que biven según razón a dar cuenta de sus negocios, mas aun tan bien del tiempo de su ocio, quanto mas los que fuemos de alcançar a ser súditos y bivir debaxo de tan poderosos y cristianíssimos príncipes, que assí artes bélicas como de paz están ya tan puestas en perfeción en estos reynos por su buena governación, que, quien piensa las cosas que por armas se han acabado, no parece aver quedado tiempo de pacificarlas como oy están.

To conclude we might now be able to answer the previous formulated question on why is Encina's *Arte de poesía castellana* so unusual for us. The answer is that Encina's work is a symptom of his awareness on the re-drawing of the public sphere. An open field where no longer there is room for 'trovadores' but 'poetas'. The poet is presented as a spectre who reveals himself before the public.

I would like to remark, in this sense, that such idea of 'poeta' embodies already what we consider in our days as 'poeta' in the strict sense. The new patronage relationships will be essential for a poet to be read, to write and to occupy a territory as an intellectual and cultural provider. It is not very distant to the institutional and governmental patronage of today, but that is another story that Encina could hardly have glimpsed.

In 1497, just one year after the publication of *Arte de poesía castellana*, Don Juan de Alba died. Encina wrote, after his death, a poem inspired by this 'sad lost' for Spain. The first verses read:

> Triste España sin ventura,
> todos te deven llorar.
> Despoblada de alegría,
> para nunca en ti tornar.
>
> Tormentos, penas, dolores,
> te vinieron a poblar.
> Sembrote Dios de plazer
> porque naziesse pesar.

As a consequence, Encina will soon lose his position in favor of Lucas Fernández. As we already know, he will move to Italy, but before that, he tries to obtain visibility by his poetic merit. In the previous verses, Encina mourns Don Juan death as leaves Spain in sorrow. José Ricardo Morales would quote these verses again, centuries later, in his poetic anthology of the exile *Poetas en el destierro* (1943). Juan del Encina had to leave Spain, and so he did. Under different circumstances, thousands of Spaniards were forced to exile centuries after. All shared the same feeling of strangeness and process of invisibilization which, regardless time and place, seems to be one of the critical features of the Spanish culture.

Works Cited

Camillo, O. (1976). *El humanismo castellano del siglo XV*. Valencia. 113.

Encina, J. del. (1978). 'Arte de poesía castellana'. *Obras completas*. Espasa Calpe. 7-8.

Lawrance, J. 2004). 'Fabulosa illa aurea saecula: The idea of the Golden Age at the Court of Isabel'. *The Spain of the Catholic Monarchs. Papers from the Quincentenary Conference*. Bristol: University of Bristol. 25-26.

Weiss, J. (1999). 'Tiempo y materia en la poética de Juan del Encina'. *Humanismo y literatura en tiempos de Juan del Encina*. Salamanca: Universidad de Salamanca. 243.

4. La habitación de Cervantes: hacia un género espectral

Todos necesitamos una 'habitación propia'. Cervantes, metafóricamente, creó la suya cuando le negaron ese espacio en el edificio de la república de las letras de su momento. A veces, lo que parece un error constituye un éxito. Cervantes encontró 'su habitación' en la innovación de un género espectral: el de la ficción novelística.

De entre los doce textos de las *Novelas Ejemplares* de Cervantes, el de 'El coloquio de los perros' es uno de los que más atención ha recibido tanto por parte de la crítica como por el conjunto de los lectores de esas obras cervantinas. Este interés se ha visto renovado a lo largo del tiempo tanto en España como en el ámbito cultural europeo.

Muchos son los aspectos de la obra que justifican esa importante consideración, pero entre ellos destacan las bases filosóficas sobre las que se asienta el texto, su alcance como reflexión metaliteraria y su papel como modelo discursivo para otros proyectos literarios, tal es la universalidad del antidogmatismo que alcanza, carácter este que además resulta una de las claves principales de toda la producción cervantina. De todo ello me ocuparé en este capítulo, en el seno del contexto literario del conjunto de las *Novelas ejemplares* y atendiendo especialmente al uso que el autor hace del 'humorismo' como elemento de subversión de los discursos establecidos en la época. Finalmente, me interesa subrayar la proyección y la trascendencia de 'El coloquio de los perros' en la literatura y el pensamiento europeo del siglo XX, aunque sea sólo señalando dos de los ejemplos más señeros.

Como punto de partida teórico me valdré del paradigma crítico que proporcionan los trabajos de A.C. Riley, 'Cervantes and Cynics (*El licenciado Vidriera* and *El coloquio de los perros*)'; de Julio Rodríguez-Luis 'Autorrepresentación en Cervantes y el sentido de *El Coloquio de los perros*'; de Jannine Montauban, 'El chiste y su relación con *El coloquio de los perros*'; de L.J. Woodward, '*El casamiento engañoso* y *El coloquio de los perros*': de Felix Carrasco, '*El coloquio de los perros*: veridicción y modelo narrativo'; de Gonzalo Sobejano, '*El coloquio de los perros* en la picaresca y otros apuntes'; de Pamela Waley, 'The unity of the *Casamiento Engañoso* and the *Coloquio de los Perros*', entre otros estudiosos y críticos.

Quizá sea un lugar común, aunque no por ello reiterar su importancia debe parecer algo innecesario, mencionar las relaciones de préstamos y de diálogos intertextuales que las *Novelas Ejemplares* presentan con respecto al *Decamerón* de Bocaccio y a los relatos de *Las mil y una noches,* cuyo compilador y traductor al árabe fue Abu abd-Allah Muhammed el-Gahshigar. Diversos y reconocidos estudiosos ya han señalado estos paralelismos de los que nos hacemos eco (Close, 2006); sin embargo hay una cuestión que no ha sido tan destacada por la crítica y que para nosotros posee mayor relevancia. Nos referimos a la hipótesis que plantea el profesor Javier Blasco (Blasco, 2005; 2006) sobre la posibilidad de que las *Novelas Ejemplares* fueran en realidad el éxito de un fracaso. Según Blasco, los textos de las *Novelas Ejemplares* fueron concebidos en principio como comedias. Como quiera que Miguel de Cervantes no alcanzó el éxito que deseara entre las compañías de cómicos y el público de los corrales, ese material no pudo ver la luz como textos teatrales directamente representables. Por ello, desde los últimos años del XVI, Cervantes comenzó a darles una forma textual y literaria diferente e innovadora, algo de lo que sabemos era consciente de acuerdo con las tan conocidas palabras de su prólogo:

> A esto se aplicó mi ingenio, por aquí me lleva mi inclinación, y más, que me doy a entender, y es así, que yo soy el primero que he novelado en lengua castellana, que las muchas novelas que en ella andan impresas todas son traducidas de lenguas extranjeras, y éstas

> son mías propias, no imitadas ni hurtadas: mi ingenio las engendró, y las parió mi pluma, y van creciendo en los brazos de la estampa (Cervantes, 2001: 19).

Efectivamente, ya por entonces Cervantes era consciente de la existencia de un mercado editorial (Rodríguez, 2003) que consumía ciertos productos y que se había mostrado especialmente abierto a lecturas como la que representaba modélicamente el *Decamerón*. De esta manera, Cervantes pudo intuir que dándole cierta unidad a las historias de las *Novelas Ejemplares* podría publicar un libro que tuviera como modelos el estilo y el formato de las 'novella' italianas y la eficacia narrativa de los 'exempla' medievales (Close, 2007; Blasco, 2005, 2006; Riley, 2001) cuyos códigos, por otro lado, eran plenamente reconocibles para un público potencial: los de la sátira didáctica (Close, 2007: 159).

A todo lo expuesto hasta ahora hay que sumar un recurso que será uno de los ejes fundamentales de una obra como *El Quijote* (Rodríguez, 2003). Se trata del juego de espejos de la literatura dentro de la literatura. 'El coloquio de los perros' mantiene una relación de dependencia con la novela ejemplar de 'El casamiento engañoso' (Waley, 1957; Woodward, 1959) a la vez que funciona como texto autónomo (Carrasco, 1986). Dicha dependencia tiene un componente doble: por un lado sirve para engarzar estructuralmente una novela con otra y por otro dotar al 'Coloquio' de una entidad narrativa que difícilmente tendría sin que su inclusión estuviera legitimada como la lectura de un texto (Rodríguez-Luis, 2003):

> —Yo me recuesto —dijo el alférez— en esta silla en tanto que vuesa merced lee, si quiere, esos sueños o disparates, que no tienen otra cosa de bueno si no es el poderlos dejar cuando enfaden (Cervantes, 1997: 264).

De la misma manera que cierra el relato con lo que bien podríamos interpretar como una reivindicación del valor último de la ficción:

> El acabar el *Coloquio* el licenciado y el despertar el alférez fue todo a un tiempo; y el licenciado dijo:
> —Aunque este coloquio sea fingido y nunca haya pasado, paréceme que está tan bien compuesto, que puede pasar el señor alférez con el segundo.
> —Con ese parecer —respondió el alférez— me animaré y disporné a escribirle, sin ponerme más en disputas con vuesa merced si hablaron los perros o no.
> A lo que dijo el licenciado:
> —Señor Alférez, no volvamos más a esa disputa. Yo alcanzo el artificio del *Coloquio* y la invención, y basta. Vámonos al Espolón a recrear los ojos del cuerpo, pues ya he recreado los del entendimiento (Cervantes, 1997: 362-363).

Las palabras con las que se cierra 'El coloquio de los perros' son clarificadoras en cuanto que hablan del papel que, para Cervantes, desempeña este texto y que no es otro que el de la articulación de una 'poética', una reflexión teórica que expone, de una forma un tanto peculiar, su punto de vista sobre en qué consiste el fenómeno de la literatura.

Por lo tanto, más que ante una mera 'sátira didáctica', como afirma Anthony Close en uno de sus más recientes estudios (Close, 2007), entiendo que la lectura más fructífera de 'El coloquio de los perros' se debe realizar desde la idea de que esta obra corresponde a una formulación teórica, filosófica y metaliteraria relativamente ajena a fines didácticos-morales.

Como A.C. Riley ya expuso en alguno de sus trabajos sobre el diálogo que mantienen los perros Cipión y Berganza (Riley, 1976; Carranza, 2003), existen en esta obra dos planteamientos filosóficos fundamentales de partida. El primero hace referencia a la elección por parte de Cervantes de la forma del 'coloquio' en el sentido que adquirió en la Edad Media, como instrumento de desarrollo de las dos caras de un mismo discurso sobre cuestiones teológicas y metafísicas. Aquella idea de que a través del enfrentamiento en forma de diálogo entre dos posiciones contrapuestas se podía producir un acercamiento a la 'Verdad', está muy presente en la configuración discursiva de 'El coloquio de los perros'. Cipión y Berganza entablan una plática que claramente proviene de dicha tradición medieval y que tomará como excusa, como pretexto, dilucidar si es posible o no que los perros puedan hablar. En este sentido el artificio cervantino es magistral, ya que no es más que un señuelo narrativo para ahondar en otras cuestiones. Tal y como Cervantes lo pone de manifiesto en el mismo comienzo cuando Cipión afirma que lo fundamental no es que simplemente 'hablen' sino que producen 'discurso'. Esta diferenciación ya nos indica, como preámbulo, el carácter esencial que tiene la palabra como principio constructivo de la ficción que al mismo tiempo es la realidad. Para Cervantes la realidad del hombre se resume en una cuestión de lenguaje, en una cuestión textual, en una cuestión plenamente discursiva:

> CIPIÓN.— Así es la verdad, Berganza; y viene a ser mayor este milagro en que no solamente hablamos, sino en que hablamos con discurso, como si fuéramos capaces de razón, estando tan sin ella, que la diferencia que hay del animal bruto al hombre es ser el hombre animal racional, y el bruto, irracional (Cervantes, 1997: 268).

A esta cuestión de la comprensión de la realidad como entidad discursiva, debemos añadirle la presencia de un componente filosófico anti-dogmático que tiene sus raíces en la doctrina de los cínicos, en Diógenes. Como es bien sabido, a Diógenes y sus seguidores los llamaban los perros (κυνικος) por su carácter desprendido y por su relajación moral. Los 'perros' vivían semidesnudos, sucios, asalvajados, sobrevivían gracias a la caridad ajena (que, al mismo tiempo que buscaban, desdeñaban) y no tenían ningún inconveniente para mantener relaciones sexuales en público (Riley, 1976; Montauban, 2009). A Diógenes se le consideraba como un 'Sócrates' que se hubiera vuelto loco, en palabras de Platón, lo que nos da una idea de la inversión de sistemas filosóficos de la que el propio Cervantes se hará eco en 'El coloquio de los perros'.

En realidad, podemos afirmar que lo que hace Cervantes es desarrollar un mecanismo literario para atacar frontalmente cualquier tipo de jerarquía o dogma. Se trata éste de un aspecto que, en buena medida, cruza todo el conjunto de la obra cervantina. La siguiente cita refrenda lo que hemos expuesto hasta ahora:

> CIPIÓN.— ¿Al murmurar llamas filosofar? ¡Así va ello! Canoniza, canoniza, Berganza, a la maldita plaga de la murmuración, y dale el nombre que quisieres, que ella dará a nosotros el de cínicos, que quiere decir perros murmuradores; y por tu vida que calles ya y sigas tu historia (Cervantes, 1997: 298).

Por ello el relato de la 'picaresca', al modo de la de *El Lazarillo de Tormes*, que rodea la historia de los dos canes en sus respectivos pasos de manos de un amo a las de otro, reafirman nuestra idea de que Cervantes se movía en un horizonte de ideas y de referencias muy claro. El simbolismo de los perros y su irreverencia podrían haberse quedado en una mera fabulación aburrida y excesivamente intelectualizada de no haber sido por la incorporación de otro elemento básico para la puesta en tela de juicio de la ideología dominante: el humor.

'El coloquio de los perros' se inicia prácticamente con un chiste que al mismo tiempo sirve como elemento desencadenante sobre la cuestión de si Cipión y Berganza pueden poseer raciocinio o no. Las líneas a las que me refiero son las siguientes:

> CIPIÓN.— Ansí es, pero bien confesarás que ni has visto ni oído decir jamás que haya hablado ningún elefante, perro, caballo, o mona; por donde me doy a entender que este nuestro hablar tan de improviso cae debajo del número de aquellas cosas que llaman portentos, las cuales, cuando se muestran y parecen, tiene averiguado la experiencia que alguna calamidad grande amenaza a las gentes.
> BERGANZA.— Desa manera, no haré yo mucho en tener por señal portentosa lo que oí decir los días pasados a un estudiante, pasando por Alcalá de Henares.
> CIPIÓN.— ¿Qué le oíste decir?
> BERGANZA.— Que de cinco mil estudiantes que cursaban aquel año en la Universidad, los dos mil oían Medicina.
> CIPIÓN.— Pues, ¿qué vienes a inferir deso?
> BERGANZA.— Infiero, o que estos dos mil médicos han de tener enfermos que curar (que sería harta plaga y mala ventura), o ellos se han de morir de hambre.

Y tras el componente humorístico viene inmediatamente el desvelamiento de los cimientos de la ideología dominante fuertemente asentada en el discurso teológico:

> CIPIÓN.— Pero, sea lo que fuere, nosotros hablamos, sea portento o no; que lo que el cielo tiene de ordenado que suceda, no hay diligencia ni sabiduría humana que lo pueda prevenir; y así, no hay para qué ponernos a disputar nosotros cómo o por qué hablamos; mejor será que este buen día, o buena noche, la metamos en nuestra casa; y, pues la tenemos tan buena en estas esteras y no sabemos cuánto durará esta nuestra ventura,

> sepamos aprovecharnos della y hablemos toda esta noche, sin dar lugar al sueño que nos impida este gusto, de mí por largos tiempos deseado (Cervantes, 1997: 269-270).

Los perros son conscientes de que se encuentran ante un portento anómalo (Montauban, 2009: 390) y, paradójicamente, esa es la primera muestra de raciocinio: la duda. La 'duda' es el principio constituyente del anti-dogmatismo. Lo primero que hacen los perros es desconfiar de la misma capacidad de la razón para mostrar una verdad irrefutable. En este sentido creo especialmente significativas las siguientes palabras de Montauban:

> Como se observa, la 'ejemplaridad' de esta novela no parece estar relacionada con el deseo de inscribirse en una supuesta tradición esópica, ni con la valoración humanista de los animales como seres capaces de ofrecer lecciones morales (como lo hicieron dos siglos después Samaniego en sus *Fábulas morales* e Iriarte en sus *Fábulas literarias*). Tampoco es usuaria de los recursos retóricos de la picaresca; la risa cumple la función de diluir la seriedad que imponen los 'valores universales', convirtiendo lo heterogéneo en una opción en sí misma. Es en esta secuencia de negaciones 'sintomáticas' que debemos leer el chiste de Berganza: cansado de escuchar la extensa perorata de Cipión acerca de si su don de habla es o no un portento (que, bien mirado, no es más que una disquisición retórica acerca de a qué 'valores universales' atentan) [...] (Montauban, 2009: 391).

Quizá lo más interesante de 'El coloquio de los perros' es que no se queda en el mero cuestionamiento de las categorías que he destacado, sino que, a lo largo de este juego retórico, finalmente enuncia una salida al peligro del relativismo absoluto, por cuyo borde Cervantes nos ha llevado sin dejarse caer en él, gracias al corpus de la casuística que los canes han ido exponiendo a través de sus experiencias vitales, que valdrán como ejemplos 'prácticos' de buen gobierno y moralidad, experiencias que nos conducen hasta la última reflexión:

> CIPIÓN.— Una muestra y señal desa verdad que dices nos dan algunos hombrecillos que a la sombra de sus amos se atreven a ser insolentes; y si acaso la muerte o otro accidente de fortuna derriba el árbol donde se arriman, luego se descubre y manifiesta su poco valor; porque, en efeto, no son de más quilates sus prendas que los que les dan sus dueños y valedores. La virtud y el buen entendimiento siempre es una y siempre es uno: desnudo o vestido, solo o acompañado. Bien es verdad que puede padecer acerca de la estimación de las gentes, mas no en la realidad verdadera de lo que merece y vale. Y, con esto, pongamos fin a esta plática, que la luz que entra por estos resquicios muestra que es muy entrado el día, y esta noche que viene, si no nos ha dejado este grande beneficio de la habla, será la mía, para contarte mi vida (Cervantes, 1997: 362).

Y es que para Cervantes la desconfianza como herramienta de conocimiento tan sólo puede desarrollarse desde la experiencia. Para Cervantes no hay teoría o pensamiento, no hay otra filosofía que la que cada individuo es capaz de desarrollar con las vivencias más elementales, tal y como es el caso de los perros Cipión y Berganza.

Como ya he mencionado en este capítulo, que no es más que una breve aproximación a ciertos aspectos presentes en 'El coloquio de los perros', esta obra ha sido objeto de interés posterior por parte de diversos escritores y pensadores. El

'Coloquio' es de por sí una pieza clave para entender la arquitectura discursiva sobre la que se emplazan los elementos principales que caracterizan su práctica literaria.

En concreto quisiera apuntar aquí rápidamente la influencia decisiva que 'El coloquio de los perros' tuvo sobre Freud y sobre Kafka. En el caso de Freud es conocida la continuada reflexión del pensador en torno a la figura de Cervantes y su obra literaria, especialmente 'El coloquio de los perros'. Sabemos por su correspondencia (Montauban, 2009) que, en su época de estudiante en la Facultad de Medicina, él mismo se hacía llamar Cipión y que a su amigo Silberstein lo denominaba como Berganza. Freud incluso llegó a fundar lo que llamó la 'Academia castellana', como así lo atestigua su extenso epistolario en español, idioma que aprendió para poder leer las obras de Cervantes en su versión original. En buena medida la sesión psicoanalítica está inspirada en el diálogo entre el alférez y el licenciado de 'El casamiento engañoso' y su desarrollo en el coloquio de los perros Cipión y Berganza.

En el caso de Kafka, su fascinación por Cervantes no es menor. En 'Informe para una academia' toma el modelo que le proporciona 'El coloquio de los perros' para enunciar su propia poética. Al modo que lo hiciera Cervantes, un mono y un domador exponen el corpus teórico desde el que Kafka considera que es posible la literatura.

A pesar de los intentos de apropiación nacionalista, Cervantes desajusta cualquier intento de lectura no espectral porque discursivamente entiende que la lectura/escritura es un proceso de descorporeización e inmersión en las posibilidades que están por acontecer y al mismo tiempo es pasado. Sus cínicos perros son espectros de un imaginario desplazado de la cultura hispánica y, me atrevo decir, europea. Tal imaginario cultural tan sólo es efectivo desde la crisis de las ideas, desde lo tentativo y transitorio. Cervantes conocía bien el 'umbral' ya que su propia vida tan sólo había sido una sucesión de estados gradualmente contigentes. La verdad relativa de esa contigencia, espectral en su esencia, es la que conforma la innovación cervantina: el vasallo que pasa a construirse como sujeto individual en la sociedad del cambio de siglo necesita de ficciones que levanten su proyecto y legitimen su posición en la narrativa cultural en quiebra del Barroco.

Para finalizar me gustaría insistir en la idea de que 'El coloquio de los perros' no es más que, a mi parecer, una comedia frustrada o, al menos, un fragmento de una de ellas. Como lo que leemos es la transcripción realizada por Campuzano, Cervantes logra convertir a sus lectores en espectadores (es decir, en 'oyentes') de ingeniosas ocurrencias orales que apuntan tanto a la creación de un modelo narrativo como a una crítica de las instituciones de poder (Montauban, 2009: 397). Cervantes era consciente de la emergencia de un nuevo público que demandaba nuevas ficciones. 'El coloquio de los perros' puede ser entendido así como una poética de un género espectral con la que anuncia un nuevo modelo literario a la vez que desmantela cualquier posición dogmática: probablemente una de las mejores y más sutiles reivindicaciones de la razón como instrumento para alcanzar la verdadera libertad de pensamiento.

Obras Citadas

Blasco, J. (2005). *Cervantes, raro inventor*. Alcalá de Henares: Centro de Estudios Cervantinos.

___. (2006). *Cervantes, un hombre que escribe*. Valladolid: Difácil.

Carranza, P. (2003). 'Cipión, Berganza and the Aesopic Tradition', en *Cervantes: Bulletin of the Cervantes Society of America*, 23.1: 141-163.

Carrasco, F. (1986). '*El coloquio de los perros*: veridicción y modelo narrativo', en *Criticón*, 35: 119-133.

Cervantes, M. (1997). *Novelas ejemplares*. Madrid: Espasa Calpe.

___. (2001). *Novelas ejemplares*, ed. de Jorge García López y estudio preliminar de Javier Blasco. Madrid: Crítica.

Close, A. (2006). *Cervantes y la mentalidad cómica de su tiempo*. Alcalá de Henares: Centro de Estudios Cervantinos.

Montauban, J. (2009). 'El chiste y su relación con *El coloquio de los perros*', en *Bulletin of Hispanic Studies*, 86: 387-400.

Riley, A. C. (1976). 'Cervantes and the Cynics (*El licenciado Vidriera* and *El coloquio de los perros*)', en *Bulletin of Hispanic Studies*, 53: 189-199.

___. A. C. (2001). *La rara invención. Estudios sobre Cervantes y su posteridad literaria*, tr. Mari Carmen Llerena. Barcelona: Crítica.

Rodríguez, J. C. (2003). *El escritor que compró su propio libro: para leer El Quijote*, Madrid: Debate.

Rodríguez-Luis, J. (1997). 'Autorrepresentación en Cervantes y el sentido de *El Coloquio de los perros*', en *Cervantes: Bulletin of the Cervantes Society of America*, 17.2: 25-58.

Sobejano, G. (1975). '*El coloquio de los perros* en la picaresca y otros apuntes', en *Hispanic Review*, 43.1: 25-41.

Waley, P. (1957). 'The unity of *The Casamiento engañoso* and *The Coloquio de los perros*', en *Bulletin of Hispanic Studies*, 34: 201-212.

Woodward, L.J. (1959). '*El casamiento engañoso* y *El coloquio de los perros*', en *Bulletin of Hispanic Studies*, 36: 80-87.

5. Breve galería hacia la modernidad: *El Sueño* espectral de Courbet o la intimidad de la mujer del XIX

A la pâle clarté des lampes languissantes,
Sur de profonds coussins tout imprégnés d'odeur,
Hippolyte rêvait aux caresses puissantes
Qui levaient le rideau de sa jeune candeur.

Femmes Damnées (Baudelaire, 1976: 152).

Hasta ahora me he centrado en aspectos que configuran la construcción de la anomalía del canon tradicional español y en obras desheradadas, o en que algún momento lo fueron, donde la expectralidad constituye un elemento fundacional. En este capítulo, me gustaría realizar una pequeña pausa. En esta casa tomada que estamos visitando hay una galería que debemos recorrer para transitar hacia la contemporaneidad. Se trata de un pasillo visual en que nos explica cómo se construyen las narrativas culturales de genéro que cruzan las apropiaciones del poder. Siempre he considerado que esta galería temporalmente se ubica en el momento finisecular, sobre todo de raigambre francesa, donde las categorías ideológicas dominantes del discurso de la burguesía en el siglo XIX restringían la presencia de la mujer en el ámbito de lo público y delimitaban un modelo muy cerrado para el de lo privado.

Sin embargo, y sobre todo en el terreno del arte, hubo diversas tentativas de superar o destruir ese horizonte ideológico. Por ello, me gustaría detenerme en una pintura específica junto con los lectores. En el cuadro *El Sueño* de Courbet y en la poesía de Baudelaire encontramos, a mi juicio, un intento de ir más allá de los límites que la sociedad burguesa imponía. Ambos autores se moverán en la frontera de la ideología burguesa, haciendo del concepto de la **transgresión** el valor central de su obra. Su posición adquirirá con el tiempo gran valor, pues no cabe duda de que iniciaron el camino que luego transitarían algunas vanguardias, especialmente el Surrealismo, u otras posiciones artísticas que se suelen reconocer bajo la denominación general de 'malditismo'.

Para analizar la obra de Courbet que lleva por título *El Sueño*, debemos fijarnos en primer lugar en dos aspectos importantes. El primero es el mismo nombre de la obra. ¿Por qué *El Sueño*? Es preciso prestar atención a los elementos que componen el cuadro y su disposición espacial. En él dos mujeres desnudas aparecen tendidas sobre una cama deshecha formando una diagonal que cruza el lienzo, desde la esquina superior hasta la esquina inferior derecha.

Una es morena y tiene un color de piel más oscuro. La otra es rubia con el pelo rizado y la carne más pálida. Sus piernas están entrelazadas produciendo una cierta sensación de movimiento y caos. Si continuamos subiendo por sus cuerpos, podemos apreciar que Courbet sólo nos muestra un brazo de cada una y el más próximo al otro cuerpo permanece oculto; mientras que el brazo libre se posa, en el caso de la rubia, sobre la pierna de la otra, en el de la morena aparece agarrando levemente un extremo del edredón caído. Es el sueño lésbico disfrutado. Se adivina en ellas un gesto placentero de sosiego tras el orgasmo.

El segundo aspecto de especial relevancia que debemos tener en cuenta para entender el cuadro es la fecha en la que Courbet realizó esta obra: 1866. En la Francia de este momento, como en Inglaterra, encontramos una sociedad patriarcal regida plenamente por los intereses y la moral de la burguesía. La mujer está destinada al ámbito de lo doméstico, lo familiar, y se elimina, a través de una serie de mecanismos creados por el discurso masculino del poder, toda capacidad de movimiento más allá de lo delimitado por el hombre. En esta coyuntura histórica no importa que una mujer sea tal, sino que se adapte lo más posible al ideal concreto de mujer que impone el pensamiento masculino dominante burgués.

La ideología masculina burguesa no concibe dentro de su discurso que la mujer pueda obtener placer sexual sin necesidad del hombre; por eso margina el lesbianismo y limita la relación sexual de la mujer al falo.

En torno a estas dos categorías ideológicas esenciales se establece el discurso pictórico o poético transgresor de Courbet y Baudelaire en los casos que estoy analizando, algo que va más allá de la mera ejecución de las formas. Ahora podemos comprender el verdadero alcance de lo que Courbet plantea. Estamos ante la búsqueda de un horizonte ideológico nuevo, hacia un nuevo arte que sustituyera todo ese mundo que tanto Courbet como Baudelaire despreciaban y que englobaban bajo el término de lo burgués.

Courbet sugiere las relaciones lésbicas entre dos mujeres, para que sea la conciencia del espectador quien termine realizando un determinado juicio de valor ante esta pintura.

El Sueño está inspirado en un poema de Baudelaire titulado Femmes Damnées incluido en *Les Fleurs du Mal*, al cual pertenece la cita con la que hemos abierto nuestro trabajo. Tanto en Baudelaire como en Courbet encontramos el aspecto común de la **transgresión** —coincidencia no casual, pues eran amigos e incluso Courbet llegó a hacer un retrato de Baudelaire— y la necesidad aguda de agredir a lo burgués porque representa un mundo que carece de valor para ellos. Sin embargo se diferencian en su concepción de la mujer.

Mientras que para Courbet la transgresión radica en el hecho de que los personajes de su cuadro son dos mujeres burguesas que viven sus relaciones lésbicas con naturalidad, sin sentir vergüenza ni conciencia de pecado, para Baudelaire la mujer es un demonio o un ángel. En concreto, Baudelaire escribirá en sus apuntes en prosa conocidos con el nombre de *Mon coeur mis à nu*, las siguientes palabras: *La femme est naturelle, c'est-à-dire abominable*.

Resulta muy interesante señalar que Courbet no entra en esta dicotomía, porque sería como permanecer en el sistema ideológico que pretende atacar. En este sentido Courbet es más moderno que Baudelaire, su planteamiento es mucho más abierto, porque inaugura un nuevo espacio para la mujer ante el horizonte ideológico burgués dominante. La dicotomía entre mujer ángel o demonio es clásica y si la admite tan bien la ideología burguesa, es porque fue una categoría cristiana desde el principio de los tiempos. Para la Iglesia la mujer siempre ha tenido algo de ángel y demonio: la mujer es la madre, Eva, pero la que nos expulsó del Paraíso por su soberbia, por su insensatez, por su tendencia natural al vicio.

Lo que Courbet dice es que pueden ser naturales a la mujer, sin ser viciosa, ciertos placeres. He aquí la posición rotundamente agresiva de este cuadro, en el que aparecen dos mujeres que en cuanto se vistan volverán al salón, a lo público, a seguir adulando los oídos de los hombres burgueses. Son reales, no son fantasías eróticas. Él presenta dos mujeres pertenecientes a la clase dominante, a la burguesía, a través de una técnica realista inspirada en el conocimiento de los clásicos —estos cuerpos podrían recordarnos perfectamente a la *Venus de Urbino* de Tiziano, cuadro éste que sí influirá directamente en la obra de otro contemporáneo de Courbet como Manet y en su Olimpia de 1865— y su canon. Con la diferencia de que, para referirse a determinadas prácticas sexuales, los clásicos del XVI y XVII hablaban de mitología o de historias bíblicas y en cambio Courbet no. Por aquí va Courbet y los siguientes párrafos pretenden ser el refrendo de lo que decimos.

Es necesario volver en este momento a la iconografía del cuadro. Las pieles están tersas y los pechos erguidos. La mujer morena tiene el rostro enrojecido como si hubiera hecho un gran esfuerzo y bajo el torso, que se gira hacia el cuerpo de la mujer rubia como queriendo atraparla, encontramos un collar de perlas que parece que se ha desprendido.

Un collar de perlas puesto en el cuello de una mujer forma un círculo, un espacio limitado que apresa simbólicamente la libertad de sus movimientos. El círculo como forma geométrica implica continuidad de un estado de cosas. Sin embargo, en *El Sueño* se nos muestra como un objeto roto que ha caído y casi como una serpiente que huye deslizándose desde la cama hacia una copa de licor.

¿Pero por qué un collar de perlas? Desde luego no es gratuita la inclusión de este elemento por Courbet. La perla simboliza la pureza, la virginidad, la virtud y, al quebrarse el círculo que formaba, el conjunto de la moral dominante masculina basada en el sistema patriarcal también ha sido destruido. Además es preciso destacar cómo ese collar nos recuerda a la forma de la serpiente que ha representado desde siempre el primer gran pecado, de la misma forma permanente que ha sido entendida como símbolo del falo.

El falo, la serpiente, el collar abandonado, contrastan con la unión placentera entre las dos mujeres. La serpiente emerge del licor; serpiente y licor forman parte de la misma sustancia, de lo prohibido para la ideología burguesa, que ésta está siendo vulnerada en este curioso juego en el que hay una clara intención de evocar lo que eran las prendas del amor clásico, realizado, satisfecho, feliz y tranquilo. De nuevo Courbet presenta la contradicción transgresora e inaguantable para lo burgués.

De este modo no nos podríamos imaginar a Delfina e Hipólita —como llama Baudelaire a las dos lesbianas que bien pudieran ser las mismas del cuadro de Courbet— leyendo, tocando el piano o pintando acuarelas como era costumbre por ejemplo en la sociedad victoriana inglesa de ese momento, pero sí a estas mujeres de Courbet, por lo que nos parece aún más innovador, aunque en ambos casos todas estas mujeres representan una vida que excede los límites: representan lo incontrolable por el ojo masculino.

Así lo que encontramos es la creación de un nuevo espacio de lo femenino, de una nueva intimidad ignota y espectral hasta ese momento para la ideología burguesa en el ámbito de lo privado. Se trata de la transgresión de una realidad establecida artificialmente a partir de las relaciones lésbicas de dos mujeres.

Por último, si regresamos a los elementos del cuadro, es importante que nos fijemos en el cabello de estas dos mujeres. Era costumbre que lo llevaran recogido, sujeto, controlado, pero aquí el pelo se derrama por los dos cuerpos que sueñan. Esa idea de dinamismo que se sugiere a través del pelo, de los cuerpos, de las manos, tiene un contrapunto en la quietud viva de las flores que rebosan el jarrón. Es fundamental señalar cómo el cromatismo de las flores y su disposición nos transmite la sensación pictórica de lo que están experimentando las dos amantes. El jarrón equilibra verticalmente, es un elemento de tranquilidad, de sosiego, de paz, que indica la ausencia del arrebato vicioso. Todo ha sido tan natural —en el sentido de normal— que hasta el jarrón con sus flores cálidas y su gama de colores amables ha permanecido intacto, perfecto, en pie. Un pasador y los pendientes reposan en el pie de la cama bajo un signo de calma.

En el otro extremo del cuadro lo que podemos encontrar es una jarra de cristal vacía y lo más importante: una sola copa. ¿Por qué estos dos elementos? La respuesta es bien sencilla. La jarra está vacía. El contenido, que sería presumiblemente licor, ha desaparecido. Courbet nos está aproximando así al estado de embriaguez de los sentidos que nos trasmiten las dos mujeres desnudas. Por otro lado tenemos la copa. Una copa de la que sale el collar de perlas-serpiente. Han bebido del mismo licor en la misma copa: el vaso embriagador de las relaciones sexuales lésbicas.

He aquí la genialidad de Courbet. De una manera sencilla, con los elementos justos y el contrapunto necesario, nos conduce a la riqueza de matices y reflexiones que he analizado.

Courbet lanza a los ojos del burgués dudas, preguntas, inquietudes, a la vez que redefine el concepto de intimidad al referirse a la mujer. No es un ser casto, no es un ser puro y angelical, es un ser desconocido porque la ideología burguesa patriarcal no escucha la voz de la mujer, sino su propia voz para definirla.

Al abrir una ventana hacia el espacio íntimo de lo femenino, Courbet introduce una nueva perspectiva sobre la mujer del XIX. Estas mujeres a las que nos referimos serán las *Femmes Damnées* situadas en los márgenes de lo diabólico y lo antinatural por la sociedad burguesa.

Me atrevo a afirmar pues que Courbet y Baudelaire coinciden en el mecanismo de transgresión, situándose en la misma posición con respecto a la ideología dominante, aunque se diferencian en la visión de la mujer. Para Courbet —al contrario que para Baudelaire— la mujer no es ni un ángel ni un demonio, es simplemente otra cosa, tan sólo un ser humano. La invisibilización de su humanidad espectraliza a la mujer y la deshereda del ámbito de lo público.

Obras Citadas

Baudelaire, Ch. (1976). *Femmes Damnées* en *Les Fleurs du Mal.* Ed. Gallimard.152.

6. La habitación de Borges: *El Otro, El Mismo* de Borges o la lógica del caleidoscopio

El otro, el mismo, publicado en 1964, es un libro de poemas en el que se pueden encontrar, a mi juicio, algunos de los elementos principales que caracterizan la producción literaria de Jorge Luis Borges, algo que en principio resulta lógico si tenemos en cuenta que los poemas que en tal libro se recogen fueron escritos a lo largo de muchos años, hasta que finalmente se reunieron dando lugar a este poemario esencial en su amplia obra.

Por ello, para cualquier acercamiento crítico a este libro es necesario que tengamos en cuenta determinados aspectos que sustentan la escritura de este conjunto de poemas preferido por el mismo autor, porque según declara en su Prólogo, 'ahí están el *Otro poema de los dones*, el *Poema conjetural*, *Una rosa y Milton*, y *Junín*, que si la parcialidad no me engaña, no me deshonran. Ahí están asimismo mis hábitos: Buenos Aires, el culto de los mayores, la germanística, la contradicción del tiempo que pasa y la identidad que perdura, mi estupor de que el tiempo, nuestra substancia, pueda ser compartido'.

Me refiero, claro está, a que es necesario rastrear las diferentes fuentes de la tradición filosófica que alimentan un discurso característico en la producción literaria de Borges. Y, entre otras, debo señalar la especial importancia de ciertas nociones de los sistemas de Heráclito, Platón y Spinoza.

La influencia de estas fuentes filosóficas no da lugar en Borges a un conjunto sistemático de nociones. A nuestro entender Borges no es un filósofo en el sentido tradicional del término y no reelabora un corpus conceptual organizado a partir de las diferentes líneas de pensamiento de los autores citados anteriormente sino que, como escritor con una visión amplia del mundo y de la vida, utiliza aquellos elementos que le sirven para expresar mejor su propia idea de la realidad y las relaciones entre las personas.

Para Borges la realidad es un conjunto de ficciones. Es un complejo entramado de situaciones, posibilidades, ambigüedades y contradicciones que nos presenta como principal problema el de su propia representación y conocimiento.

Por eso debo apuntar antes de seguir adelante cuáles son las ideas de esos filósofos que influyeron en Borges. En primer lugar, según Heráclito la vida es un continuo fluir circular en el que al cabo de un tiempo los hechos vuelven a repetirse. Por otro lado, para Platón existen una serie de arquetipos, de formas puras, pertenecientes al ámbito de lo *Divino*, al que las formas degradadas del mundo real deben ascender en una purga continua a lo largo del tiempo hasta alcanzar ese estado primigenio.

Estas dos ideas están muy presentes en el pensamiento de Borges. Para el autor del *El otro, el mismo*, la realidad es como un caleidoscopio. Es decir, lo real existe dentro de un cierto límite en el cual un conjunto de elementos van cambiando de forma y lugar. Como en un caleidoscopio, el contorno serían los límites del conocimiento y las piezas y las figuras que se forman a través del artificio de los espejos explican de un modo metafórico la realidad.

Así se puede entender el interés de Borges por esas nociones que antes señalábamos brevemente y que da título a este capítulo: la lógica del caleidoscopio. Sin embargo, el pensamiento de Borges va más allá y para ello se vale de la teoría de Spinoza, que afirma básicamente que el ser humano no tiene acceso a la sustancia en sí sino al constructo con el que el pensamiento representa la sustancia. En las palabras de lo que he ido exponiendo en las páginas de este libro, la concepción ficcional de Borges es esencialmente espectral.

De ahí que sólo a partir de la duplicidad de un objeto que es a la vez otros, de las formas de un caleidoscopio, se pueda llegar a un cierto conocimiento de la realidad. *El otro, el mismo* resume bien esta idea ya desde su título, como señala con acierto el filósofo Fernando Savater con las siguientes palabras:

> La trama misma de la obra de Borges no tiene más que un motivo central, repetido inagotablemente: la duplicación. Esencial duplicidad de Borges. La literatura es el doble del mundo real, que acaba por sustituir a éste, de tal modo que ya no podemos saber si hubo alguna vez tal cosa como un "mundo" fuera de la creación literaria. Inacabable juego literario de las duplicaciones: palabra y cosa, forma y contenido, significante y significado, argumento y estilo, autor y personajes, invención y observación, ética y estética, ficción y reportaje... Cada uno de estos términos parece definirse por relación al otro, que se le opone; un examen más profundo revela que todos los atributos del uno corresponden al otro, con un cambio de nivel y una diferencia de énfasis. Constatamos dos mundos superpuestos, paralelos, que la memoria (o ese tipo especializado de memoria, el pensamiento) unifica. Leer o vivir; el tigre cantado y el que no está en el verso... Borges no tiene otro tema que éste de la doble factura del mundo, precisamente porque su único secreto es la literatura o, mejor dicho, su secreto y el de la literatura son el mismo. Todo Borges puede resumirse en el título de unos de sus libros: El otro, el mismo (Savater, 1992: 209-210).

El hecho de que Borges se aproxime a estos filósofos anteriores a la Ilustración no es una casualidad. Para entenderlo hay de tener en cuenta que el discurso literario de Borges se encuentra enmarcado dentro de un contexto histórico concreto. En aquellos años de la primera mitad del siglo XX en Argentina, una literatura de corte realista, que respondía a un programa de elaboración de una conciencia nacional argentina, es la tendencia dominante. El discurso literario de Borges es una reacción contra esta corriente que prevalecía en ese momento y que representaba, a su juicio, toda una serie de valores hueros. Es decir, el discurso de Borges no es suprahistórico, pero sí que realiza una selección dentro de la tradición filosófica occidental, para desmarcarse de una literatura simplona que reproducía el tópico con la intención de crear así una identidad nacional argentina.

El gran hallazgo de Borges no es la producción de una literatura de evasión o de la fantasía, sino que confiere al concepto de realidad una dimensión dual, dinámica y abierta. La realidad es cambiante por definición, como lo es un caleidoscopio. De ahí la deliberada ambigüedad de sus poemas o el juego con el equívoco. Para Borges tan sólo se puede tener una cierta conciencia de la realidad a partir de lo que podríamos llamar la lógica de la contradicción, es decir, de ese juego continuo que surge a partir del reflejo entre las fichas del interior de un caleidoscopio y los espejos.

En otros términos lo que ocurre en el discurso que elabora Borges, en mi opinión, es que el yo del Estado y el yo de la Subjetividad no forman parte de dos niveles distintos de la realidad. Desde una perspectiva diferente a la de Borges, el yo del Estado estaría sujeto a una serie de convenciones para que el colectivo funcione y por otro lado, el yo de la Subjetividad no necesitaría de esas reglas para actuar, puesto que se concibe como intrínsecamente libre, y remitiría por lo tanto a otro nivel de comprensión, de representación de la realidad. Sin embargo para Borges estos límites caen, se hacen difusos o desparecen como ahora veremos.

A nuestro entender Fernando Savater explica bien lo que sucede en la literatura de Borges en un artículo que anteriormente citábamos y del que ahora necesitamos reproducir otro fragmento:

> Lo que ocurre es que Borges ha sido particularmente incapaz de sustentar la convencional distinción literaria entre el discurso del mundo y el mundo mismo, que

> en un cierto plano —que Hegel llamaba plano del entendimiento— es indispensable para el normal funcionamiento del Estado, lo que ha situado su escritura a un nivel tan implacablemente realista, que el sentido común (es decir, la interiorización de la Ley) no puede ya verlo como tal y le adscribe al género fantástico o la evasión. Todo el patetismo contenido de Borges reside, sencillamente, en su declarada incapacidad para alcanzar el otro tigre, el que no está en el verso; pero esta incapacidad no es prueba de su escapismo sin retorno a lo fabuloso, sino de su realismo, porque ese tigre que no está en el verso no existe (1992: 208).

La caída de la distinción literaria de la que nos habla Savater no es más que la reelaboración de un viejo problema filosófico, que antes mencionaba, como lo es el de las representaciones y la distinción entre el yo del Estado y el de la Subjetividad. Acerquémonos ahora al siguiente poema que Borges escribe sobre Spinoza y que transcribimos completo dada su brevedad:

> Spinoza
>
> Las traslúcidas manos del judío
> Labran en la penumbra los cristales
> Y la tarde que muere es miedo y frío.
> (Las tardes a las tardes son iguales.)
> Las manos y el espacio de jacinto
> Que palidece en el confín del Ghetto
> Casi no existen para el hombre quieto
> Que está soñando en su claro laberinto.
> No lo turba la fama, ese reflejo
> De sueños en el sueño de otro espejo,
> Ni el temeroso amor de las doncellas.
> Libre de la metáfora y el mito

> Labra un arduo cristal: el infinito
> Mapa de Aquél que es todas Sus estrellas (1995: 88).

Borges escoge una escena perfecta para expresar la preocupación central de la filosofía de Spinoza: el orfebre que labra un objeto libre de la realidad de la literatura (*libre de la metáfora y el mito*), es decir, no sujeto a los límites de la representación, da forma al infinito, a la sustancia en sí, que no es ni más ni menos que Dios. Felipe Martínez Marzoa se refiere en los siguientes términos al pensamiento de Spinoza en su *Historia de la Filosofía*:

> Para Spinoza, la "definición" de una figura no consiste en unas características que la distingan estáticamente de toda otra (como: circunferencia es una línea cuyos puntos están todos a una misma distancia de otro dado), sino en la construcción —la génesis— de la figura (p.ej.: la circunferencia se produce por el movimiento de un segmento manteniendo fijo uno de sus extremos). Lo verdadero, para Spinoza, es presente en el entendimiento en el sentido de que es construido —de que se produce— en el entendimiento; no es simplemente "percibido", sino concebido; su presencia no es simplemente perceptio, sino conceptus (1971: 98-99).

Esta es la cuestión que está latiendo en *El otro, el mismo* y que podemos encontrar a lo largo de sus poemas. A mi juicio la composición que lleva por título *Límites* representa bien lo que hasta ahora he venido explicando.

Como vemos en esos versos, los límites de lo real y de lo que no es real son para Borges deliberadamente ambiguos y sólo a partir de esas contradicciones se puede tener una cierta conciencia de la existencia misma. El espacio y el tiempo dejan de poseer importancia como absolutos; al contrario, cobran vida y están sujetos al cambio como cualquier otra idea perteneciente a un discurso creado por los seres humanos. En *Límites* se respira un cierto sentimiento de nostalgia, de caminar irremediablemente hacia el olvido, de ausencia y resignación, *Creo en el alba oír un atareado/ rumor de multitudes que se alejan;/ son lo que me ha querido y olvidado...*Borges se referirá a este poema con el siguiente comentario:

> [...] Y otro poema que me gusta es "Límites". Pero creo que puedo decir el motivo. El motivo es, supongo, que es bastante fácil escribir un poema original, digamos, con una idea original o sorprendente. En fin, si se piensa un poco, eso fue lo que hicieron los poetas metafísicos en Inglaterra, ¿no? Pero en el caso de "Límites" he tenido la gran suerte de escribir un poema sobre algo que todo el mundo siente, o puede sentir. Por ejemplo, lo que siento hoy en Cambridge; mañana salgo para Nueva York y no regresaré hasta el miércoles o jueves y siento que hago las cosas por última vez. Y así, creo que la mayor parte de los sentimientos comunes, la mayor parte de los sentimientos humanos, han encontrado forma dentro de la poesía, y expresados una y otra vez, como debe ser, durante el último milenio Pero en este caso tuve mucha suerte, porque teniendo tras de mí un largo período literario, o sea, habiendo bebido en muchos literatos, parece que he encontrado un asunto que es lo suficientemente nuevo y, sin embargo, no es demasiado extravagante. Porque cuando digo, especialmente a cierta edad, que estamos haciendo las cosas por última vez y que tal vez no somos conscientes de ello, porque, por lo que sé, puede que esté mirando por esta ventana por última vez, o que hay libros que nunca leeré, libros que ya he leído por última vez, creo que con esto abro, digámoslo así, la puerta a un sentimiento que todos los hombres tienen. Y desde luego otros poetas lo hacen mil

> veces mejor que yo, pero éste había sido uno de los primeros poemas sobre este tema. Así que tengo bastante suerte, como si fuese el primer hombre en escribir un poema sobre la alegría de la primavera o la tristeza del otoño (Burgin, 1974).

Efectivamente, Borges no se aleja de la realidad sino que reelabora su carácter contingente, le da el valor de un discurso que crea la subjetividad y que se modifica constantemente. Fernando Savater comenta lo siguiente al respecto:

> Su confinamiento en la literatura no aleja a Borges de esa confusa abstracción, la "realidad". Por el contrario, le sitúa en el corazón de la realidad o, mejor, en la realidad de la realidad. El haber advertido que el discurso es la realidad de la realidad hace de Borges el escritor más moderno[...] En verdad, hasta muy recientemente no se ha revelado plenamente esa condición nuclearmente real de lo literario, que posibilita la escritura de Borges. Por "literario" no hay que entender solamente lo que es habitual considerar narración o poesía, sino también esas otras formas poéticas o narrativas que son la filosofía, la teología, la teoría científica, las constituciones políticas o las proclamas revolucionarias. Es perfectamente obtuso seguir insistiendo en el carácter ficticio e inventado de lo literario, por oposición a la condición de real y de dado que se supone al hipotético mundo efectivo. Precisamente lo literario es lo que realmente se nos da en cada momento, lo que condiciona moralmente nuestras acciones, lo que nos explica científicamente cuál es la "verdad" de lo que nos rodea, lo que nos crea una identidad y un nombre propio, lo que configura nuestros arrebatos amorosos o nuestras urgencias políticas. La misma distinción entre palabras y cosas, entre teoría y praxis,

> entre literatura y mundo real, es perfectamente literaria. Las invenciones y fingimientos comienzan precisamente cuando intentamos posesionarnos de lo "natural" o volver a la primordialidad de la "vida real" pues, incapaces de abandonar la órbita de lo literario, vamos haciendo cada vez pero literatura, más vaga y divagatoria, más llena de recursos a lo "inefable" o de términos desesperadamente abstractos, como "ahí", "esto", "ahora"... (1994: 207).

Por ello debemos prestar especial atención a lo que Borges señala en otro poema, el titulado *Arte Poética.* Ese poema ilustra bien todas las ideas que hasta ahora hemos expuesto. Borges define en el poema la escritura de la poesía como *Convertir el ultraje de los años/ En una música, un rumor y un símbolo*. Por eso el discurso literario de Borges está construido a través de unos símbolos muy concretos que sirven para dar forma a las nociones abstractas que previamente hemos analizado. Estos símbolos constituirán las piezas del caleidoscopio, un vehículo de representación de la realidad. Es aquí donde encontramos de una manera expresa a Heráclito, no sólo porque cite su nombre en el penúltimo verso, sino porque esa noción del tiempo como un continuo fluir circular que al principio señalábamos está aquí representada por la imagen del río que es *tiempo y agua.*

De este modo vayamos a esos símbolos de los que hablábamos, esos fragmentos del caleidoscopio que representan la realidad. Los símbolos de la literatura borgeana son prolijos así que, debido a la extensión a la que debe ceñirse este trabajo, hemos seleccionado sólo dos de entre los que creo más representativos. Estos son el Golem y los Espejos, que a su vez dan título a dos poemas que forman parte de *El otro, el mismo.*

El primer símbolo que vamos a estudiar es el del Golem. En *El Golem* encontramos un discurso sobre un discurso, es decir, el discurso de la *Creación* inserto en el discurso de la *creación*. Borges elimina la división entre lo absoluto y lo relativo haciendo que el poema sea ambas cosas al mismo tiempo. La creación de un Golem por un rabino está sugerida como la creación del hombre por Dios; para que nos entendamos, una cadena infinita de creaciones imperfectas que se yuxtaponen en el tiempo y el espacio hasta llegar a la categoría de Dios, quien se nos presenta como algo ambiguo, como un rabino que pudiera sentir compasión por su Golem. El Golem —ese simulacro de hombre— es un símbolo de Borges porque, aunque originariamente provenga de la tradición cabalística judía, él lo usa como un elemento que le ayude a la representación de su discurso, la representación de la realidad. No podemos olvidar lo que el propio Borges comentará sobre este poema:

> Borges: Pues sí; creo que mi mejor poema es uno llamado "El Golem". Porque "El Golem", bueno, Bioy Casares me dijo que es un poema donde el humor tiene su parte. Y entonces el poema es más o menos un relato de cómo evolucionó el Golem y hay una especie de parábola porque uno piensa en el Golem como algo torpe ¿no?, y el rabino está bastante avergonzado de él. Y al final se sugiere que lo que el Golem es para el mago, para el cabalista, así el hombre es para Dios, ¿no? Y que tal vez Dios se avergüence de la humanidad como el cabalista se avergüenza del Golem. Y creo que en ese poema se puede encontrar también una parábola sobre la naturaleza del arte. Aunque el rabino intenta algo hermoso, o muy importante, la creación de un hombre, sólo consigue crear un muñeco bastante torpe, ¿no? Una especie de parodia humana (Burgin, 1974: 95-96).

El otro poema que he escogido y que, a mi entender, constituye uno de los símbolos característicos de la literatura de Borges (el espejo), es el titulado *Los Espejos.*

La dualidad que personifica el espejo o la representación de la realidad con la que percibimos el mundo, está perfectamente encarnada en el juego de reflejos del interior del caleidoscopio. Por eso Borges dirá *Que haya sueños es raro, que haya espejos,/ Que el usual y gastado repertorio/ De cada día incluya el ilusorio/ Orbe profundo que urden los reflejos.* Borges se refiere a una realidad cambiante, un mundo de formas que varían, pero sobre la forma fija que da el contorno del caleidoscopio o, en otras palabras, de Dios.

Algunos críticos han querido entender la escritura de Borges como un discurso de evasión frío y matemático, donde no hay margen para la experiencia. Saúl Yurkievich mantiene lo siguiente al respecto:

> Tras sus vacilaciones iniciales, Borges asume, cada vez con mayor nitidez, la postura de clásico. Ella coincide con su personalidad, más permeable al incentivo filosófico que al sensorial. Pocas veces sus poemas nacen de estímulos sensibles; más frecuentes son los literarios o las resonancias emotivas de una idea. De su obra podemos extraer una autobiografía intelectual; difícilmente la sentimental y anecdótica. Hay en él una consciente emulación de los modelos canónicos, porque a toda originalidad la considera ilusoria (1971: 122).

No puedo más que disentir con lo que Yurkievich afirma. Pienso que Borges nos descubre tanto nuestra relación con el mundo como a nosotros mismos, nos plantea una aventura de descubrimiento a través de las formas literarias y de su lectura, precisamente el carácter eminentemente real de su literatura, siempre que entendamos lo real como una construcción de entendimiento de la sustancia, a la que no podemos tener acceso en sí, como decía Spinoza.

Lo que no resulta Borges es exageradamente sentimental o anecdótico, sino que con mesura introduce determinados elementos de todas sus vivencias. Para Borges no hay distinciones entre lo filosófico y lo sensorial; este autor está más allá del tópico que relaciona lo frío y lo matemático frente a lo sentimental y lo literario. Por eso utiliza elementos de la filosofía para expresarse literariamente. Todo le interesa porque forma parte del mundo, de ese inmenso caleidoscopio que intentamos descifrar en esta aventura de auto-conocimiento que es la vida. ¿Acaso no hay estímulo más sensible que el de la lectura de un libro y lo que nos sugiere?

En Borges, la literatura como discurso, los nombres y los autores que cita, todos son elementos que el propio autor elaboró a lo largo del conjunto de su obra en un afán de búsqueda para encontrar una manera de representar la realidad, una lógica, la que he denominado en este capítulo *lógica del caleidoscopio*.

En otras ocasiones se ha acusado a Borges de ser demasiado *clásico*. A mi juicio, si se le puede relacionar con la imitación de los modelos clásicos, ha de hacerse en el sentido renacentista de la *imitatio*, porque conoce que sólo desde un conocimiento amplio de la tradición puede innovarse, que ser original (como etimológicamente indica la palabra) es relativo o perteneciente a los orígenes, es decir, de alguna manera volver a los orígenes, la Ítaca del poema *Límites* por ejemplo.

Fernando Savater da su parecer también sobre cómo la crítica muchas veces ha errado en sus juicios en torno a la escritura de Borges, otorgándole etiquetas no muy acertadas como la de escribir una literatura irracional, de evasión y otros tantos términos alejados de lo que, a mi entender, expresan sus palabras y sus libros:

> Borges paga su terca radicación en la función literaria con el aura de caprichosa irrealidad que rodea su obra, la cual le gana la admiración de espíritus débiles, que han hecho de la superfluidad bandera poética, y la animadversión de quienes abundan tanto en problemas reales que nunca se plantean la realidad como problema. Es un malentendido inevitable, probablemente irrelevante, pues los malentendidos son el tejido mismo de la lectura. ¿Deberé insistir, tras estas páginas, que nada hay más ajeno al disciplinado y realista Borges que el capricho o la irrealidad? Es inútil, pues muy pocos me creerán y él nunca disipará el equívoco (1994: 214).

En conclusión debo señalar que, si bien Borges no es un filósofo sistemático, su discurso literario si está construido a partir de las teorías filosóficas que explicaba al comienzo de este estudio. Como hemos tenido oportunidad de comprobar en *El otro, el mismo* confluyen los temas que Borges desarrolla en el conjunto de su obra literaria. Al contrario de lo que muchos piensan, Borges no meparece un escritor alejado de la vida y los sentimientos, sino que su poesía aborda ciertos problemas de la existencia a través de un discurso que disuelve los límites entre el yo de lo público y el de lo privado. La realidad, para Borges, no es más que un constructo sujeto al azar del presente y de la historia que fija Dios, al igual que lo es todo lo que tiene que ver con el ser humano. Borges no puede comprender la vida, la realidad, sino como la lógica de un caleidoscopio donde el individuo está condenado a perderse y encontrarse para siempre.

Obras Citadas

Alazraki, J. (1988). *Borges and the Kabbalah and other essays on his fiction and poetry.* Cambridge University Press.

___. (1977). *Versiones. Inversiones. Reverciones. El espejo como modelo estructural del relato en los cuentos de Borges.* Madrid: Gredos. 132-144.

Annick, L. (1997). *Jorge Luis Borges: oeuvre et manoeuvres.* Paris: L'Hartmattan. París.

Barnatán, M.R. (1972). *Borges.* Madrid: Espasa.

Barrenechea, A.M. (1965). *Borges. The Labyrinth maker.* New York University Press.

Borges, J.L. (1995). *Obras Completas. El otro, el mismo.* Barcelona: Círculo de Lectores. Emecé.

___. (1972). *Obra Poética. El otro, el mismo.* Madrid: Alianza/Emecé.

Bosco, M. A. (1967). *Borges y los otros.* Compañía General Fabril Editora. Argentina.

Burgin, R. (1974). *Conversaciones con Jorge Luis Borges.* Madrid: Taurus.

Cahiers L'herne. (1964) *Jorge Luis Borges.* París.

Cohen, J.M. (1973). *Jorge Luis Borges.* Oliver and Boyd. Edimburgh. 99-103.

Di Giovanni, N. T.; Halpern, D.; Mcshange, F. (1974). *Borges on writing.* London: Penguin Books.69-103.

Ferrer, M. (1971). *Borges y la nada.* London: Tamesis books. 83-106.

Foucault, M. (1966). *Les mots et les choses. Une archeologie des sciences humaines.* Paris: Gallimard.

Freidemberg, D. *'El poeta imposible'*. *Borges Studies on Line.* J. L. Borges Center for Studies & Documentation. Internet: 14/04/01 (http://www.hum.au.dk/romansk/borges/bsol/df1.htm)

González Echeverría, R. (1972). '*With Borges in Macondo*'. *Diacritics.* Vol.II. 57-60.

Martínez Marzoa, F. (1973). *Historia de la filosofía. Filosofía moderna y contemporánea.* Istmo. Madrid.

Pezzoni, E. (1999). *Lector de Borges. Lecciones de Literatura. 1985-1988.* Sudamericana. Buenos Aires.

Rodríguez Monegal, E. (1976). *Borges, hacia una lectura poética.* Madrid: Ediciones Guadarrama.

Rodríguez, J.C. (2002). *¿De qué hablamos cuando hablamos de literatura .Versiones sobre Borges.* Granada: Comares. 293-397.

Running, T. (1996). *The critical poem. Borges, Paz, and Other Language- Centered Poets in Latin America.* London: Bucknell University Press.

Savater, F. (1994). '*Borges: Doble contra sencillo*'. *La infancia recuperada.* Madrid: Santillana.

Sucre, G. (1966). *Borges, el poeta.* Monte Ávila Editores. Caracas.

Teobaldi, D. G. *La memoria del origen. Algunos aspectos de la poesía de Jorge Luis Borges.* (http://www.ucm.es/info/especulo/numero8/borg_teo.htm)

Vian, C. (1980). *Invito alla lettura di Borges.* Mursia. Milano. 129-137.

Yurkievich, S. (1971). *Fundadores de la Nueva Poesía Latinoamericana: Vallejo, Huidobro, Borges, Neruda, Paz.* Barcelona: Seix Barral.

7. Lorca's room: the spectral woman and *Doña Rosita la Soltera*

The spectral metaphor is especially useful for explaining processes of (in)visibilization of marginal communities or individuals. Federico García Lorca (1898-1936) was a writer who understood, to a very important extent, the role of literature as a power source to provide visibility to those who were both neglected or ignored by the 'otra mitad', as he said in many occasions, or, in other words, those who suffered the unbalances of a society progressively based on social and economic inequality.

One could argue that Federico García Lorca is an over-revisited author. Indeed the bibliography we have on Lorca's works is witness to confirm such an assertion. However, there are still substantial gaps to be fulfilled in terms of the critical approach to his works, the reception of his texts and the attention that some of his writings require as, for instance, are the cases of his prose book entitled *Impresiones y paisajes* or, that which will be the focus of my interest in this meditation, the drama *Doña Rosita la Soltera o El Lenguaje de las Flores*.

Impresiones y paisajes has been narrowly framed as a mere first attempt full of mistakes and imperfections. *Doña Rosita la Soltera* does not escape from a limited outlook too. It has been traditionally assessed about the so-called 'rural trilogy' (*Bodas de Sangre*, *Yerma*, and *La Casa de Bernarda Alba*) and defined by some critics just as a 'prosaic portrayal of the lonely descent into spinsterhood' (Nickel, 1984: 522). In my opinion, both works have been relegated to a secondary level for different reasons, which flow into a general misconception on considering Lorca's writings only as the result of his homosexuality, his folklore concern and his relationships among the members of the so-called 'Generation of 1927'.

As I have demonstrated in another of my works[3], Lorca's literary project was very far from the mystified and accepted image of a young genius without a proper knowledge of the literary traditions that wrote by merely following some kind of 'magical-duende' instincts. Far from this, Lorca had a vast culture and a deep knowledge of the different literary discourses he decided to affiliate. It is relevant to note as well the essential process of literary learning that Lorca maintained all his life; especially acute when in 1917 he devoted himself to literature as he pointed out in one of his early writings:

> Los sacerdotes, ebrios del vino y de la lujuria, clamaron "Sursum Corda", creyendo hacer creer para ellos… pero los corazones no se movieron. Todo que-

---

[3] See Pablo Valdivia (2007), 'Impresiones y paisajes: Un libro epigonal del simbolismo español', en Ángel Esteban, *Darío a Diario. Rubén y el Modernismo en las dos orillas*. Granada: Universidad de Granada. 235-254: '*Impresiones y paisajes* ha recibido muy poca antención por parte de la crítica especializada. Sólo recientemente ha empezado a dejar de ocupar una posición marginal en el amplio interés que sigue mereciendo el conjunto de la obra literaria de Federico García Lorca. Hasta ahora se ha tildado ese libro como un trabajo de meros tanteos lleno de erratas: una serie de ejercicios que emulaban algunas de sus lecturas o unas páginas que mostraban su sentimiento juvenil de músico frustrado. Tales presupuestos apuntalan la imagen más tópica del autor granadino, la del mártir de la guerra civil, el héroe homosexual de los gitanos, el genio rebelde irreverente o el vanguardista atrevido de las bromas de la Residencia de Estudiantes. Independientemente de que la enorme potencia de su figura mítica haga que siempre acudan a nuestra memoria *Bodas de Sangre*, *Poeta en Nueva York* o *Mariana Pineda* antes que *Impresiones y paisajes*, es evidente que la diferente altura intelectual y artística de las obras más conocidas de Lorca ha contribuido también a mantener estos olvidos; no sólo el mito consigue que vengan rápidamente estos títulos y no otros a nuestro pensamiento'.

> dó envuelto en la bruma de la muerte y, mientras, los apóstoles, andando por los bosques, por las mares, por las noches de lo desconocido. ¡Ay!, Dios mío, dame fuerzas para poder hablar muy alto con el corazón henchido de piedad. No me des desfallecimiento y languideces. No me sumas en la indiferencia espiritual. Derrama sobre mí tu misericordia. ¡Ay! Dios mío del Bien, del Amor y de la Pasión. ¿Qué hay de nosotros en la confusión infinita…?
> Final
> Miserere mei, Deus, secundum magnam misericordiam tuam.
>
> Noche de 15 de octubre de 1917.
> Federico. 1 año que salí hacia el bien de la literatura (Maurer, 1998).

My approach will that take into consideration such a process of learning as I have just described, to get beyond the overinterpretations, which are commonplace in much-studied authors as Lorca. My understanding considers possible to trace individual literary dialogues between Lorca's texts and different texts to which Lorca had access. For instance, as the remains of Lorca's library show us, or the readings he quoted in interviews and letters, as well as other cultural manifestations that brought his attention. On this active consideration of his work, it is especially exciting and fruitful to have open eyes to what Lorca is saying to us rather than projecting a reading or a priori into his lines.

Unhappily, many times, criticism has become a practice which replaces with anecdotes or gossips the actual exercise of reading texts and many approaches have dropped into several forms of banality. Perhaps this tendency is one of the reasons why the general categories that I mentioned before succeeded over the small literary categories and why has been poorly studied the process of obtaining an own literary voice. How many studies have we read on his relation with Dalí or Buñuel? Instead, who knows, except the indirect reference by the biographers or the seminal research of Gallego Morell, anything about Martín Domínguez Berrueta. These are some of the contradictions I would like to stress about Lorca's critical assessment.

In this sense, I can talk about of how a particular myriad of readings of Lorca's writings has been profusely and compulsively carried out following the myth previously described. It is one of the reasons why the Lorca's texts, which did not follow the orthodox myth described by some critics, are still barely known. The second reason, apparently, is the different quality of each text. Nonetheless who may define *Libro de poemas* or *Doña Rosita la Soltera* as bad pieces of literature? The truth is they have not received the same attention as works as *Mariana Pineda*, for instance, which fulfills all the categories assigned traditionally to Lorca's works. The case of *Mariana Pineda* is especially relevant as it is, from the action developed at the scene, an entirely horrible play. Lorca still didn't know at that time how to carry out a drama. The rich language of the text saves the play, but even he does not do the essential elements of the dynamism of the scene. Nevertheless, it is one of the most recognized plays as it touches a topic, which fulfills some political expectations projected on Lorca's work by the general reception of his literature. Indeed a civic engagement is present in many Lorca's texts, it is always essential to underline the revolutionary meaning that most of his works had at this time, but the overinterpretation of his works from this approach has created false stereotypes, such as those of Lorca as a communist writer or, the opposite, assuming he was just the spoiled offspring of a wealthy family.

Fortunately, *Impresiones y paisajes* and *Doña Rosita la Soltera* escape such reductionism because they did not fit so well in Lorca's criticism preconceptions. Consequently, they have been marginalized at all levels, from research to teaching. If one compares the number of studies published on *Doña Rosita la Soltera* and the number of interests received by *La Casa de Bernarda Alba*, *Yerma* or *Bodas de Sangre*, the statistics show quite clearly how poorly *Doña Rosita* has been studied.

Some critics have argued *Doña Rosita la Soltera* insists on displaying some common topics which appear in other Lorca's dramas such as the struggle between fertility and sterility, the frustration, the time passing by, the mockery of certain affected customs and manners, among others. We cannot neglect that in *Doña Rosita*. To some extent, this is true. Nonetheless, still what has not been reached is, from my approach, the 'raison d'être' of this play: the dramatic development of an *aporia*. I suggest this is so because of an intrinsic problem of traditional critics considering drama criticism as mere analysis of the text leaving aside the fact that every written play is a performance proposal, in other words, forgetting that the book is a point of departure to be fulfilled by the acting and the scene composition.

By the time Lorca wrote *Doña Rosita* he had already overcome all his problems on how to compose a drama. He knew how to use the different rhythms, how to introduce movement through words and, the most important aspect, how to seduce the attention of the audience by the factual performance well accompanied with measured, poetic language. The reflection made by him on the play entitled *El Público* is essential in this sense to my view.

In my opinion, there was a crucial moment when Lorca realized that the audience was the key to a drama. At that moment, at the beginning of the 30's, he read the Greeks and Latin masterpieces (Camacho, 2006) and he understood that all his writings were under the frame of the Greek inheritance. In this context, the idea of *El Público* aroused. Lorca proposed himself to get over the Greek model, to go beyond it. And he did it. 'El Teatro Bajo la Arena' is not a model of drama conceived only to make a public announcement of his homosexuality or a projection of it, as some critics have pointed out. From my approach, it represents a whole new drama model suggested to get over his tradition. I could argue from my perspective that *El Público* was to some extent the manifesto and *Doña Rosita* was the put into practice of this radical new appraisal of drama. Let's read the following quote[4]:

> Director
> Caballeros…
>
> Hombre 1º
> Sí, sí. Director del teatro al aire libre, autor de Romeo y Julieta.
>
> Hombre 2º

---

[4] Federico García Lorca (2000), *El público*. Madrid: Alianza Editorial. 49-51. See following extract: Hombre 1º: ¿El señor Director del teatro al aire libre?/ Director: Servidor de usted./Hombre 1º: Venimos a felicitarle por su última obra./Director: Gracias./Hombre 3º: Originalísima./Hombre1º:¡Y qué bonito tútulo! Romeo y Julieta./ Director: Un hombre y una mujer que se enamoran./Hombre 1º: Romeo puede ser un ave y Julieta puede ser una piedra. Romeo puede ser un grano de sal y Julieta puede ser un mapa./ Director: Pero nunca dejarán de ser Romeo y Julieta./Hombre1º: Y enamorados. ¿Usted cree que estaban enamorados?/ Director: Hombre… Yo no estoy dentro…/Hombre1º:¡Basta!¡Basta! Usted mismo se denuncia./ Hombre 2º (Al Hombre 1º) Ve con prudencia. Tú tienes la culpa. ¿Para qué vienes a la puerta de los teatros? Puedes llamar a un bosque y es fácil que éste abra el ruido de su savia para tus oídos. ¡Pero un teatro!/ Hombre 1º: Es a los teatros donde hay que llamar; es a los teatros, para…/Hombre 3º: Para que se sepa la verdad de las sepulturas./Hombre 2º: Sepulturas con focos de gas y anuncios y largas filas de butacas.//

¿Cómo orinaba Romeo, señor Director? ¿Es que no es bonito ver orinar a Romeo? ¿Cuántas veces fingió tirarse de la torre para ser apresado en la comedia de su sufrimiento? ¿Qué pasaba, señor Director, cuando no pasaba? ¿Y el sepulcro? ¿Por qué al final no bajó usted las escaleras del sepulcro? Pudo usted haber visto un angel que se llevaba el sexo de Romeo, mientras dejaba el otro, el suyo, el que le correspondía. Y si yo le digo que el personaje principal de todo fue una flor venenosa, ¿qué pensaría usted? Conteste.

Director
Señores, no es ése el problema.

Hombre 1º
No hay otro. Tendremos necesidad de enterrar el teatro por la cobardía de todos y tendré que darme un tiro.

Hombre 2º
¡Gonzalo!

Hombre 1º (Lentamente)

Tendré que darme un tiro para inaugurar el verdadero teatro, el teatro bajo la arena.

Director
Gonzalo…

Hombre1º
¿Cómo?... (Pausa)

Director (Reaccionando)
Pero no puedo. Se hundiría todo. Sería dejar ciegos a mis hijos y luego, ¿qué hago con el público? ¿Qué ha-

> go con el público si quito las barandas al Puente? Vendía la máscara a devorarme. Yo vi una vez a un hombre devorado por la mascara. Los jóvenes más fuertes de la ciudad, con picas ensagrentadas, le hundían por el trasero grandes bolas de periódicos abandonados, y en América hubo una vez un muchacho a quien la máscara ahorcó colgado de sus propios intestinos.

The lack of *referentiality* is the critical issue here. It is criticism towards some drama tendency on representing the world as it is dismissing it, for the sake of the audience, the metaphorical and suggestive power of the words at the theatre. Lorca was moving in a horizon of paradoxes. On one hand the dramas, which gained success, referential, linear, very happy with *conservativism* or self-pleased with its model. On the other side, the way to escape the mentioned horizon was the return to the classics, which was not a permanent solution, as a new way of representation of the world was needed, in Lorca's opinion. Lorca, as I think I have sufficiently explained, was in the middle of this intersection of different paths.

La Casa de Bernarda Alba, *Yerma*, and *Bodas de Sangre* follow the Greek pattern with the particularity that language, the extraordinary language that Lorca elaborates, is resulting in very rare originality where futurist metaphors are recognized by the audience as close to them at the same time as they are brand new. But in *Doña Rosita* he is advancing further. Defining them in a metaphorical way *La Casa de Bernarda Alba* is a razor meanwhile *Doña Rosita* is a slow internal process of destruction and, what is even more amazing, understood as something ordinary by its main character.

It is necessary to add something else. Lorca, being on this extraordinary modern, he was proposing a drama model too when wrote the play. He had the help, for many years, of Rivas Cheriff and Eduardo Ugarte until he understood that as he declared in an interview:

> El teatro es la poesía que se levanta del libro y se hace humana. Y al hacerse, habla y grita, llora y se desespera. El teatro necesita que los personajes que aparezcan en la escena lleven un traje de poesía y al mismo tiempo que se les vean los huesos, la sangre. Han de ser tan humanos, tan horrorosamente trágicos y ligados a la vida y al día con una fuerza tal, que muestren sus traiciones, que se aprecien sus olores y que salga a los labios toda la valentía de sus palabras llenas de amor o de ascos. Lo que no puede continua res la supervivencia de los personajes dramáticos que hoy suben a los escenarios llevados de las manos de sus autores. Son personajes huecos, vacíos totalmente, a los que solo es posible ver a través del chaleco un reloj parado, un hueso falso o una caca de gato de esas que hay en los desvanes. Hoy en España, la generalidad de los autores y de los actores ocupan una zona apenas intermedia. Se escribe en el teatro para el piso principal y se quedan sin satisfacer la parte de butacas y los pisos del paraíso. Escribir para el piso principal es lo más triste del mundo. El público que va a ver cosas queda defraudado. Y el público virgen, el público ingenuo que es el pueblo, no comprende cómo se le habla de problemas despreciados por él en los patios de vecindad. En parte tienen la culpa los actores. No es que sean malas personas, pero… «Oiga, Fulanito –aquí un nombre de autor-, quiero que me haga usted una comedia en la que yo… haga de yo. Sí, sí; yo quiero hacer esto y lo otro. Quiero estrenar un traje de primavera. Me gusta tener veintitrés años. No lo olvide.» Y así no se puede hacer teatro. Así lo que se hace es perpe-

> tuar una dama joven a través de los tiempos y a una galan a despecho de la arteriosclerosis (Lorca, 1998).

As mentioned at the start Lorca's works need to be assessed in the singularity of each text, poem, line, and word, as well as a whole because the process of learning and the mindful critical meditation is in his conception of the writings. I must remind the reader of some ideas expressed by Lorca:

> El teatro fue siempre mi vocación. He dado al teatro muchas horas de mi vida. Tengo un concepto del teatro en cierta forma personal y resistente (Lorca, 1998).

Lorca's reflections on the technique of drama are alive in his works. Let's consider now *Doña Rosita la Soltera* from this point of view and how Lorca achieved to draw at the scene the personal contradiction of someone: Rosita, who was singular and universal, desired freedom and accepted her drama at the same time.

To contextualise *Doña Rosita la Soltera* within Lorca's literary production I would like to briefly set out a summary of some of the texts where we could find previous traces. Mario Hernández located the atmosphere which forged *Doña Rosita la Soltera* by arguing that:

> No se puede entender el surgimiento de Doña Rosita sin esa ambigua actitud que recorre fugazmente poemas, ensayos y declaraciones de Lorca, Aleixandre, Dalí, Gómez de la Serna o Neruda. Con fecunda agudeza Ramón define la nueva visión en su capital "Ensayo sobre lo cursi", que todos pudieron leer en una revista generacional, Cruz y Raya (Hernández, 1998: 40).

Daniel Devoto in his article 'Doña Rosita la Soltera: estructura y fuentes' established an early French publication as Lorca's touchstone aesthetic discourse on the language of the flowers. This book is entitled *Nomenclature raisonnée des espèces varietés et sous-variétés du genre rosier* published in Paris in 1818, written by Aug. de Pronville, which Lorca knew thanks to José Moreno Villa during a conversation with him, Pepín Bello and Dalí.

We cannot forget as well the importance of Pedro Soto de Rojas' definition of the interior garden, or texts written by Lorca as *Tragicomedia de don Cristóbal y la señá Rosita*, poems from *Canciones* and *Libro de poemas*; verses as the ones we read in the poem 'Elegía a Doña Juana la Loca':

> Princesa enamorada sin ser correspondida [...]
> Soñabas que tu amor fuera como el infante
> que te sigue sumiso recogiendo tu manto.
> Y en vez de flores, versos y collares de perlas
> te dio la Muerte rosas marchitas en un ramo (Lorca, 1998: 58).

Or in this extract from 'Deseo':

> Sólo tu corazón caliente,
> y nada más.
>
> Mi paraíso un campo
> sin ruiseñor
> ni liras,
> con un río discreto
> y una fuentecilla (Lorca, 1998: 183).

Or the following fragment in 'Meditación bajo la lluvia':

> Ha besado la lluvia al jardín provinciano

> dejando emocionantes cadencias en las hojas.
> El aroma sereno de la tierra mojada
> inunda el corazón de tristeza remota (Lorca, 1998: 189).

Indeed, traces of his original concern about women's frustration and the realm of the affected aesthetics of the 'cursi' are in all the texts mentioned. However, I would like to stress specially a passage from *Impresiones y paisajes* where I believe it is rooted, maybe in an unconscious way, probably not, what later will be *Doña Rosita la Soltera o el Lenguaje de las Flores*:

> Sobre las nubes había suavidades de rosas transparentes…En un esquinazo del paseo, entre rosales blancos y grandes matas de dompedros, unos novios se hablaban juntando las cabezas con ansia visible de besarse… Algunas mozuelas los miraban envidiosas de reojo… ¡Bien merecía la tarde cargada de lujurias celestes, un beso apasionado de aquellos amantes!... En un banco de piedra gris con brillos de espejo, una vieja apergaminada y roñosa entretenía un bebé rubio que manoteaba ansiosamente queriendo cortar una rosa que temblaba serena entre el ramaje… (Lorca, 1998: 184-185).

From *Impresiones y paisajes* Lorca already focus his interest in that 'beso apasionado de aquellos amantes' that Doña Rosita will never obtain. Rosita was one of that 'mozuelas' who wanted to reach freedom, to be whoever they wanted to be out of the constrictions imposed by the society.

Doña Rosita will reveal in the final part of the drama where the originality of this text lies which consists in a strange balance between humor and sadness, irony and compliment, affected aesthetics and actual values, Doña Rosita's fatality and the acceptance of her destiny. As I proposed before here, we face a difference about other Lorca's dramas. None shouts or screams in *Doña Rosita la Soltera* as in *La Casa de Bernarda Alba*; none dies in a passion fight of knives under the moonlight as in *Bodas de Sangre*, none kills her partner as a projection of her frustration as in *Yerma*. It is relevant to pay attention to some extracts from his famous plays:

> Bernarda
> Y no quiero llantos. La muerte hay que mirarla cara a cara. ¡Silencio! (A otra Hija.) ¡A callar he dicho! (A otra Hija.) ¡Las lágrimas cuando estés sola! Nos hundiremos todas en un mar de luto. Ella, la hija menor de Bernarda Alba, ha muerto virgen. ¿Me habéis oído?¡Silencio, silencio he dicho!¡Silencio! (Lorca, 2002: 205).

> Novia
> ¡Porque yo me fui con el otro, me fui! (Con angustia) Tú también te hubieras ido. Yo era una mujer quemada, llena de llagas por dentro y por fuera, y tu hijo era un poquito de agua de la que yo esperaba hijos, tierra, salud; pero el otro era un río oscuro, lleno de ramas, que acercaba a mí el rumor de sus juncos y su cantar entre dientes (Lorca, 1998: 162).

> Yerma
> Marchita, marchita, pero segura. Ahora sí que lo sé de cierto. Y sola. (Se levanta. Empieza a llegar gente.) Voy a descansar sin despertarme sobresaltada para ver si la sangre me anuncia otra sangre nueva. Con el cuerpo seco para siempre. ¿Qué queries saber? No os acerquéis, porque he matado a mi hijo. ¡Yo misma he matado a mi hijo! (Lorca, 2003: 123-124).

Bernarda who commands silence, the Bride who exposes here personal drama as a Greek heroine and Yerma who affirms 'Marchita, marchita, pero segura' have a close end from the dramatic point of view. Death cuts and destroys everything. The tragedy eliminates the possibility for any other possibilities. Far from this we find Rosita's internal painful *aporia* as the worst unsealed wound than any Lorca's female character has ever suffered. The following extract will illustrate what I have just explained:

> Rosita
> Me he acostumbrado a vivir muchos años fuera de mí, pensando en cosas que estaban muy lejos, y ahora que estas cosas ya no existen sigo dando vueltas y más vueltas por un sitio frío, buscando una salida que no he de encontrar nunca. Yo lo sabía todo. Sabía que se había casado; ya se encargó un alma caritativa de decírmelo; y he estado recibiendo sus cartas con una ilusión llena de sollozos que aun a mí misma me asombraba Lorca (Lorca, 1998: 148-149).

It is here in that 'Yo lo sabía todo' where the aporia plays its role. In other Lorca's plays there is always an outer world which constraints the characters that divide the public and private sphere. However, in Doña Rosita they are unified by this 'Yo lo sabía todo', she is not a Greek heroine struggled by the Fate. Federico García Lorca, explained quite accurately in an interview who really is Doña Rosita:

> -Dime Federico; ¿qué es Doña Rosita?
> -Doña Rosita es la vida mansa por fuera y requemada por dentro de una doncella granadina, que poco a poco se va convirtiendo en esa cosa grotesca y conmovedora que es una solterona en España. [...] Poema para

> familias, digo en los cartels que es esta obra, y no otra csa es. ¡Cuántas damas maduras españolas se verán reflejadas en doña Rosita como en un espejo! He querido que la más pura línea conduzca mi comedia desde el principio hasta el fin. ¿Comedia he dicho? Mejor sería decir el drama de la cursilería española, de la mojigatería española, del ansia de gozar que las mujeres han de reprimir por fuerza en lo más hondo de su entraña enfebrecida (Hernández, 1998: 27).

I must underline the words Lorca is using: 'vida mansa' / 'vida requemada'; 'grotesca' / 'conmovedora'. It is a comedy apparently because it precisely hides what a drama is. The pain of many women who lived in an aporia due to her sexual repression. That 'reprimir por fuerza' is the engine of the play by absence. Repression is not performed in the drama, but it is present in Doña Rosita, who is her repressor and the victim at one time.

'Yo lo sabía todo' those words make us shudder. Doña Rosita declares that she knew that were no hope to recover her love or to avoid her situation. Lorca locates us into this *aporia* from the very beginning of the play. We just need to pay attention to the title *Doña Rosita la Soltera*. 'Doña' is referred in Granada to women who are married or are widows; 'Rosita' is the diminutive of 'Rosa' and it is used when we refer to someone young. Then if someone is a 'Doña', hardly could be 'soltera'. An adjective eliminates the logical possibility of the other. The contrast, within the Granada's collective understanding, appeals to a spinster, an old spinster that only could be called as Doña Rosita.

I would like to contextualize my analysis by bearing in mind what Mario Hernández asserts in his remarkable prologue to *Doña Rosita la Soltera* in the Alianza edition. It is relevant to remind that…

> En esa sociedad del XIX y principios del XX la soltería femenina lindaba con el mal absoluto, con la derrota de las ilusiones esenciales, con el truncamiento del ser de la mujer. Un "catecismo para las muchachas" de época romántica (1841) trazaba las líneas inequívocas de la vida femenina desde la primera juventud, casi desde la adolescencia.

The social impositions in the provincial space of Granada's turn of the century were the perfect field to develop Rosita's drama because, in ideological terms, Granada represented for Lorca the battlefield between the ideals of the Enlightenment, radically expressed within the discourse of the Positivism, and the progressive proposal of the modernist artists (Unamuno, Machado, Azorín, among others) who attempted to regenerate Spain through culture clearly influenced by the project of the Institución Libre de Enseñanza. A similar idea could be traced in Carlos Arniches' *La señorita de Trevélez* who states that only by the education the country will be saved from the 'señoritos'. This 'farsa' was highlighted at the moment (1914) as a work about 'regeneracionismo'. Marañón said this was for him one of his favorite plays. He defined it as a 'comedian hondamente triste aunque provoque la risa'.

What Lorca describes is how a new ideology based on a Positivist thought is winning the match to a naïve thinking rooted in the world of the spiritual, the language of the flowers, which is double-faced: the affected 'language of the flowers' embodied on one hand by Rosita's uncle and on the other hand the old figure of Martín, who represents the ideals of the Institución Libre de Enseñanza. In the middle of that two different discourses, we find a character like Doña Rosita condemned to suffer inside the disjoints of the society. A society portraited by Lorca with irony and humour as well as with bitter sadness. As the 'Ama' describes 'la sangre corre por debajo de las venas, pero no se ve'. It is precisely the engine of this drama: a silent contradiction that only produces deep despair. In the following extract, Doña Rosita performs such paradox mainly with the clarifying sentence of 'No quiero ver cómo pasa el tiempo'. People and daily life are only the ones who provide memories of what is going beyond her 'self-*aprisionamiento*' which is, in the end, a dialectic process. She pleases herself because of the constrictions of society believing that it is the right thing to do:

> Tía
> ¿Estás contenta?
>
> Rosita
> No sé.
>
> Tía
> ¿Y eso?
>
> Rosita
> Cuando no veo a la gente estoy contenta, pero como la tengo que ver…
>
> Tía
> ¡Claro! No me gusta la vida que llevas. Tu novio no te exige que seas hurona. Siempre me dice en las cartas que salgas.
>
> Rosita
> Pero es que en la calle noto cómo pasa el tiempo y no quiero perder las ilusiones. Ya han hecho otra casa nueva en la placeta. No quiero enterarme de cómo pasa el tiempo.
>
> Tía

> ¡Claro! Muchas veces te he aconsejado que escribas a tu primo y te cases aquí con otro. Tú eres alegre. Yo sé que hay muchachos y hombres maduros enamorados de ti.
>
> Rosita
> ¡Pero, tía! Tengo las raíces muy hondas, muy bien hincadas en mi sentimiento. Si no viera a la gente, me creería que hace una semana que se marchó. Yo espero como el primer día. Además, ¿qué es un año, ni dos, ni cinco? (Lorca, 2000: 102-103).

But life, inevitably, passes by as the example of Martín Domínguez Berrueta shows us…

The character of don Martín has been considered by critics as a caricature. In Edwards study on Lorca's dramas this will be argued with great conviction:

> Don Martín, el viejo profesor de colegio que aparece ahora en escena, es otra figura en la que se plasma el tema del paso del tiempo. […] En algunos aspectos, el personaje de Don Martín resulta, sin duda, una figura cómica. Su pelo rojo y la muleta son detalles físicos que poseen todo el grosor de una caricatura. Y el recitado de unos versos de una obra de teatro claramente mala que él escribiera contrasta con su genuina afición por la cultura y resulta de una gran incongruencia cómica […] Don Martín es una reliquia del pasado. Pero lo que es aún más importante: Don Martín, a quien se ha negado el amor en la vida y que no ha tenido ante sí sino los años que han ido pasando, es la imagen de lo que Rosita terminará siendo (Edwards, 1983: 308-309).

Such reading of don Martín's character seems quite problematic to me. We face here the case of something which Lorca did in other plays like *La Casa de Bernarda Alba* or *Bodas de Sangre*. Some of the characters are inspired by reality. He distorted them superficially but always taking into consideration a previous plan. Don Martín was don Martín Domínguez Berrueta, professor of the Theory of the Arts and Literature who mentored him when Lorca joined his lessons and helped him to publish his first writings in different newspapers around Spain. The same writings that, after being reviewed, were an essential part of his first published book: *Impresiones y paisajes*. Don Martín represents an old language, but his figure and what he ideologically incarnates is treated with great affection. It is a homage to what he did in the past. The crutches are a symbol or reminiscence of what that over honeyed world was missing.

It seems very strange to me the fact traditional criticism has not mentioned this before. Lorca's first book was meant to be called *Caminatas por la España Vieja* and may have contained a prologue by don Martín himself. As a result of different disagreements, Lorca and don Martín broke their friendship. However, long time after don Martín is dead Lorca stressed the massive debt he owed to his mentor and emphasized what that book, written in the context of the 'Viajes Pedagógicos' promoted by don Martín, represented for him as his first step in the path of literary expression.

In my opinion, don Martín is treated with nostalgia tending to irony rather than with mockery. Furthermore, he represents an unknown world that he embraces in Doña Rosita by paying tribute to his attempt to implement the knowledge and the cultural background of the pupils in provincial society. On the other hand dozens of 'Señor X' started to appear, whose arrogance, as a reflection of their ignorance, dismissed a naïve ideology, a naïve language indeed, but which proposed, at least (here is where we see the real nostalgia) a counteract to the blind faith in the progress embodied by 'Señor X': pompous character who tries to patronise everyone through his lessons. Lorca will see in the character of Don Martín the representative of an ideology which has failed but which Lorca safeguards as he describes don Martín like 'un tipo noble, de gran dignidad, con un aire de tristeza definitiva'; meanwhile the gift of 'Señor X' represents what Lorca rejects from modernity. Señor X's gift to Rosita illustrates my assertion:

> El Señor X
> Le entrega usted de mi parte este *pendentif*. Es una Torre Eiffel de nácar sobre dos palomas que llevan en sus picos la rueda de la industria (Lorca, 1998: 90).

Don Martín is inspired in a real person, but at the same time, he is the product of distortion as I said. An element is added to such misuse. He includes in a non direct way someone who was a main figure in Lorca's youth. I refer to Antonio Segura Mesa, one of Lorca's music teachers who wrote an unsuccessful 'operetta' entitled *Las Hijas de Jephté*, never performed, and which is assigned in *Doña Rosita la Soltera* to the character of Don Martín. The following passages confirm my analysis:

> El señor X (Con el pie puesto en la silla y jugando con el bastón)
> Superlativamente; aunque un catedrático de Economía Política no puede discutir con un cultivador de rosas. Pero hoy día, créame usted, no privan los quietismos ni las ideas oscurantistas. Hoy día se abren camino un Juan Bautista Say o Se, que de ambas maneras suele y puede decirse, o un conde León Tolstuá, vulgo Tolstoi, tan galán en la forma como profundo en el concepto. Yo me siento en la Polis viviente; no soy partidario de la Natura Naturata.

The ideology of Positivism faces the project of Institución Libre de Enseñanza inspired in the figure of Martín Domínguez Berrueta:

> Martín
> Mi vida de siempre. Vengo de explicar mi clase de Preceptiva. Un verdadero infierno. Era una lección preciosa: "Concepto y definición de la Harmonía" (Lorca, 1998: 137).
>
> Martín
> No sé por qué escribo, porque no tengo ilusión, pero sin embargo es lo único que me gusta. ¿Leyó usted mi cuento de ayer en el segundo número de *Mentalidad Granadina*? (Lorca, 1998: 141).

Or in another example:

> Martín
> No se le da hoy mérito a la Retórica y Poética, ni a la cultura universitaria.
>
> Tía
> ¡Qué le vamos a hacer! Ya nos queda poco tiempo en este teatro.
>
> Martín
> Y hay que emplearlo en la bondad y sacrificio (1998: 143).

'Bondad' and 'sacrificio' were keywords in the 'institucionista' language. Those words appear in Sanz del Río's *Ideal de la humanidad para la vida.*

I understand that Lorca pays tribute, and does not mock of don Martín Domínguez Berrueta. Although he doesn´t assume don Martín's ideas and finds them outdated, Lorca pays tribute to what the discourse of renovation brought to the provincial Granada at that time. I consider that an accurate reading of this drama cannot be done without taking into consideration the context I have just described.

Despite *Doña Rosita la Soltera o el Lenguaje de las Flores* has been poorly studied it is, in my opinión, an essential landmark in Lorca's work because of its profound analysis on some topics already drawn in his first book *Impresiones y paisajes*. Meanwhile *La Casa de Bernarda Alba*, *Yerma*, *Bodas de Sangre* o *El Amor de don Perlimplín con Belisa en su Jardín* are works which launched a heartbreaking cry of denounce against the repression of the most natural and pure drives, in *Doña Rosita la Soltera* Lorca succeeded in creating a drama of 'sangre para adentro', a tragedy which makes the audience smile because of the ridiculous, affected manners of the provincial bourgeois but which at the same time make us suffer from the extreme sadness of Doña Rosita who accepted the contradiction of her role in the society. In that sense the dialogue maintained between the Ama and the Tía is entirely clear:

> Ama
> ¿Y ya está? ¿Usted sentada y yo sentada?¿ Y a morir tocan? ¿Y no hay ley? ¿Y no hay gábilos para hacerlo polvo…?
>
> Tía
> Calla, ¡no sigas!
>
> Ama
> Yo no tengo genio para aguantar estas cosas sin que el corazón me corra por todo el pecho como si fuera un

> perro perseguido. Cuando yo enterré a mi marido lo sentí mucho, pero en el fondo una gran alegría...; alegría no..., golpetazos de ver que la enterrada no era yo. Cuando enterré a mi niña... ¿me entiende usted?, cuando enterré a mi niña fue como si me pisotearan las entrañas, pero los muertos son los muertos. Están muertos, vamos a llorar, se cierra la puerta, ¡y a vivir! Pero esto de mi Rosita es lo peor. Es querer y no encontrar el cuerpo; es llorar y no saber por quién se llora; es suspirar por alguien que uno sabe que no se merece los suspiros. Es una herida abierta que mana sin parar un hilito de sangre, y no hay nadie, nadie en el mundo, que traiga los algodones, las vendas o el precioso terrón de nieve (1998: 134).

Another book, *Impresiones y paisajes*, will be present in *Doña Rosita* as a point of departure and a growing presence of the tribute which pays to the forgotten figure of his university mentor, the professor Martín Domínguez Berrueta.

Lorca re-elaborates and models materials which already pre-existed in his works to give them a brand new form of such an emotive and intellectual depth that probably this may be the cause for why it has been displaced to a secondary stage, strangely undervalued by academic criticism. The poor don Martín, writer never laureated, flower which dies in a provincial city, mentor of Lorca and champion the ideas of the Institución Libre de Enseñanza belongs to that strange kind of human beings as Doña Rosita who pays the prize of asking what no one wants to hear:

> Rosita
> Ya soy vieja. Ayer le oí decir al ama que todavía podía yo casarme. De ningún modo. No lo pienses. Ya perdí la esperanza de hacerlo con quien quise con toda mi SANGRE, con quien quise y... con quien quiero. To-

> do está acabado… y, sin embargo, con toda la ilusión perdida, me acuesto, y me levanto con el más terrible de los sentimientos, que es el sentimiento de tener la esperanza muerta. Quiero huir, quiero no ver, quiero quedarme serena, vacía… (¿es que no tiene derecho una pobre mujer a respirar con libertad?). Y, sin embargo, la esperanza me persigue, me ronda, me muerde; como un lobo moribundo que apretara sus dientes por última vez (1998: 149-150).

However, what it is fascinating for me is how the essential question in Lorca's literary discourse '¿es que no tiene derecho una pobra mujer a respirar con libertad?' will reject any heroism in *Doña Rosita la Soltera.* What makes the difference is Rositas's universality as she explains:

> Rosita
> Sería el cuento de nunca acabar. Yo sé que los ojos los tendré siempre jóvenes, y sé que la espalda se me irá curvando cada día. Después de todo, lo que me ha pasado le ha pasado a mil mujeres (1998: 151).

I must stop now by stressing the fundamental question Lorca pointed out: '¿es que no tiene derecho una pobre mujer a respirar con libertad?'. Doña Rosita broadened Lorca's literary universe. Doña Rosita, not a martyr, not a hero, just a woman who desires to have the chance to choose her own path. The question, thanks to its aporetical and universal dimension and aim in the play, it is still without an answer. Lorca knew it: indeed tragedies are beyond any easy resolution and, by nature, are the consequence of our collective and personal contradictions: 'el cuento de nunca acabar'.

Works Cited

Camacho, J.A. et alii. (2006). *La Tradición Clásica en la Obra de Federico García Lorca*, ed. José María Camacho Rojo. Granada: Universidad de Granada.

Edwards, G. (1983). *El teatro de Federico García Lorca*. Madrid: Editorial Gredos.

García Lorca, F. (1998). 'Impresiones y paisajes', ed. Rafael Lozano Miralles. Madrid: Cátedra.

___. (1998). *Prosa Inédita de Juventud*, ed. Christopher Maurer. Madrid: Cátedra.

___. (1998). *Libro de poemas*. Madrid: Alianza Editorial.

___. (1998). *Bodas de Sangre*, ed. Allen Josephs y Juan Caballero. Madrid: Cátedra.

___. (2000). *El público*. Madrid: Alianza Editorial.

___. (2003). *Yerma*, ed. Mario Hernández. Madrid: Alianza.

___. (2002). *La Casa de Bernarda Alba*, ed. Allen Josephs y Juan Caballero. Madrid: Cátedra.

___. (1998). *Doña Rosita la Soltera o El lenguaje de las flores*, ed. Mario Hernández. Madrid: Alianza.

Hernández, M. (1998). 'Prólogo a Doña Rosita la Soltera o el Lenguaje de las Flores' Federico García Lorca, *Doña Rosita la Soltera o el Lenguaje de las Flores*. Madrid: Alianza Editorial.

Nickel, C. (1984). 'The function of Language in García Lorca's Doña Rosita la Soltera', *Hispania*. 522.

Valdivia, P. 'Impresiones y paisajes: Un libro epigonal del simbolismo español', en Ángel Esteban, *Darío a Diario. Rubén y el Modernismo en las dos orillas*, Granada: Universidad de Granada.

8. La habitación de Morales: exilio y espectralidad[5]

Si existe el caso de un escritor español que ejemplifique los rasgos más significativos de lo que hemos expuesto hasta ahora en este libro, ése es, sin duda, José Ricardo Morales (1915). Morales, como bien señalara Manuel Aznar Soler, encarna a la perfección el drama del exiliado ya que no sólo fue despojado de su tierra al término de la Guerra Civil española sino que además le fue arrebatada toda posibilidad de siquiera poder tener un público con el que su obra pudiera entrar de manera franca y directa.

De manera extensa, me he ocupado de la figura pública de Morales y de sus obras en diversos trabajos pero sobre todo en mi libro *José Ricardo Morales, de mar a mar: teatro transnacional, exilio y periferia* (2014). Sin embargo, hay un aspecto que hasta ahora no he podido tratar extensamente: la espectralidad como noción historiográfica que explica la conflictiva relación que Morales, como también sucede con otros autores exiliados, ha mantenido con el Canon tradicional español.

Para comenzar, quisiera evocar en el pensamiento del lector una imagen muy importante tomada en el año 1935 en Valencia. En ella aparecen los miembros de *El Búho*, la compañía de teatro creada por las iniciativas estatales de la Segunda República, que fue dirigida por Luis Llana, Max Aub y, posteriormente, por el propio Morales. Esa imagen del grupo de teatro de *El Búho* —ligado a la FUE y a la Universidad de Valencia— adquiere, con el paso de los años, un halo sobrecogedor, ya que de todas las personas que ahí aparecen, tan

[5] Este capítulo fue publicado como artículo en la revista *Laberintos* tal y como se indicó al comienzo de este libro. He considerado oportuno incluirlo también en este libro como capítulo porque es el lugar para el que originariamente fue concebido.

sólo José Ricardo Morales aún sobrevive[6]. El pasado se hace presente. De cierto modo ese Morales pasado nos apela como un espectro para que no olvide el espectador presente cómo el franquismo destruyó todos los intentos que se había conformado hasta 1939 por adecentar, en lo posible, la escena cultural española. De ahí que resulten más escalofriantes aún si cabe las palabras de José Ricardo Morales cuando en uno de sus ensayos sobre el destierro declaraba que aquellos jóvenes de la foto tan sólo les quedaron tres opciones cuando se fraguó la derrota de la República: estar enterrados, aterrados o desterrados.

Esta imagen a la que aludo se complementa con otra imagen evocada por Max Aub en las páginas del *Teatro español sacado a la luz de las tinieblas de nuestro tiempo* (1973). En la Academia de la Lengua ficticia que compone Max Aub en su ficticio discurso de entrada en esta institución, José Ricardo Morales aparecerá como uno de esos autores —junto con Fernando Arrabal y Antonio Buero Vallejo, entre otros— que aún no tenían silla por falta de ellas pero que en el futuro ocuparían un lugar destacado en el Canon de las letras españolas.

En realidad, la Academia descrita por Aub en ese texto es una Academia poblada por espectros: García Lorca, Machado o Juan Ramón Jiménez, por mencionar algunos nombres. Es aquí donde ambas imágenes se abrazan en el salto de 1935 a 1973, 33 años más tarde, y donde se ejemplifica, de manera muy clarificadora a mi entender, el carácter espectral de la literatura española contemporánea.

Como todos sabemos, Lorca fue asesinado por razones políticas nada más comenzar la Guerra Civil, Machado murió enfermo al cruzar la frontera de Francia mientras huía del fascismo y Juan Ramón Jiménez, tras haber estado cerca de per-

[6] En el momento en el que escribí este artículo, Morales todavía vivía. Morales falleció poco después de cumplir los 100 años.

der la vida en Madrid, moriría a mediados de la década de los cincuenta en Puerto Rico. Ése era el Canon que dejaba el franquismo al desmantelar y aniquilar la república de las letras españolas anterior a 1939: un espacio lleno de fantasmas.

En este contexto de ideas destaca especialmente un volumen de José Ricardo Morales titulado *Fantasmagorías*. El día 2 de agosto de 1981, en la página 7 del periódico *Las últimas noticias* publicado en Santiago de Chile, aparecía un artículo de prensa firmado por Floridor Pérez en el que se anunciaba la aparición del volumen *Fantasmagorías* de José Ricardo Morales en el seno del catálogo de la editorial universitaria de la Universidad de Chile.

Como ya he explicado en diversos trabajos sobre la dramaturgia de Morales (Valdivia, 2011; 2013a; 2013b; 2013c; 2014), la biografía y la recepción de la obra de José Ricardo está conformada, en cierto sentido, por una acumulación de 'destiempos' (Godoy Gallardo, 2000, 2001, 2003, 2007; Monleón, 1969, 1970, 1973, 1992). Sin embargo, *Fantasmagorías* surgió justo en el momento único e irrepetible en el que la Facultad de Ciencias Físicas y Matemáticas de la Universidad de Chile financió un conjunto de publicaciones y de actividades que transcendían los estrictos límites académicos que han dividido el saber en ciencias vs. artes. El propio autor de la noticia muestra su sorpresa ante este hecho al manifestar lo siguiente:

> "El autor agradece la publicación de este libro a la Facultad de Ciencias Físicas y Matemáticas..." (¡) ¿Es que las fantasmagorías han empezado aquí, una página antes del prólogo? No. A poco andar se justifica esta solidaridad, ya que la ciencia aporta en buena medida los conflictos dramáticos del teatro de Morales, mientras la técnica monta la desoladora escenografía en que deambulan sus personajes (Pérez, 1981: 7).

Por tanto, como bien se apunta en el texto, *Fantasmagorías* se publica en un extraño y singular instante cuando todavía está presente en el mundo académico, al menos en el de la Facultad ya mencionada, una concepción humanística del saber similar a la que también vertebra el teatro de Morales como indagación incesante sobre la naturaleza humana. Otra confluencia temporal de *Fantasmagorías* se encuentra en la coincidencia de la publicación del volumen con la del cuadragésimo aniversario de la fundación de la compañía Teatro Experimental de la Universidad de Chile, en la que Morales dirigió la primera obra puesta en escena por ese grupo (Valdivia Milla, 2010).

He insistido en otros estudios sobre la importancia que tiene para la escena teatral chilena el hecho de que Morales trasvasara parte del repertorio de El Búho, aquel otro grupo de teatro universitario en el que Morales inició su andadura teatral en la España republicana antes de la Guerra Civil. Así, el 22 de junio de 1941, el Teatro Experimental de Chile representó *Ligazón* de Valle-Inclán, cuyo subtítulo es el de 'Auto para siluetas' (Valdivia, 2011; 2013a; 2014).

Sin duda, ya en esta obra de Valle-Inclán anida un principio de 'espectralidad' muy anterior al enunciado por Jacques Derrida en *Espectros de Marx* (1993) y que marcó lo que Esther Peeren y María Pilar Blanco denominaban en su *Espectralities reader* (2013) como el giro espectral, es decir, el cambio de dirección en los estudios humanísticos hacia la consideración de lo 'espectral' como categoría de análisis social, cultural e histórico.

De alguna manera, la representación de *Ligazón* y la publicación de *Fantasmagorías,* paradójicamente y a pesar de estar alejadas en el tiempo, comparten un mismo espacio, un mismo paradigma esencial dentro de las preocupaciones y de los intereses estéticos e intelectuales de José Ricardo Morales. En las próximas páginas de este estudio se analizará este volumen compuesto por cuatro obras dramáticas de Morales en relación con la categoría de 'espectralidad' propuesta por el propio autor en el prólogo, que claramente anticipa y enriquece las propuestas de Derrida de 1993.

Marx, durante el proceso de escritura de *El Manifiesto Comunista*, dudó sobre la conveniencia de denominar ese texto con el título *Espectros*, ya que consideraba que el poder y las manifestaciones humanas encierran un carácter espectral que las define. Según la última edición del Diccionario de la Real Academia Española de la Lengua, un espectro se define como un 'fantasma (imagen de una persona muerta)'. A su vez, si nos remitimos a la palabra 'fantasma', este mismo diccionario nos informa que el término 'fantasma' proviene del latín 'phantasma' y éste, a su vez, del griego 'φάντασμα'. Entre sus posibles acepciones el Diccionario da cuenta de las siguientes:

> 1. m. Imagen de un objeto que queda impresa en la fantasía.
> 2. m. Visión quimérica como la que se da en los sueños o en las figuraciones de la imaginación.
> 3. m. Imagen de una persona muerta que, según algunos, se aparece a los vivos.
> 4. m. Espantajo o persona disfrazada que sale por la noche para asustar a la gente.
> 5. m. Persona envanecida y presuntuosa.
> 6. m. Amenaza de un riesgo inminente o temor de que sobrevenga.
> 7. m. Aquello que es inexistente o falso.
> 8. m. Población no habitada.

Si examinamos con detenimiento todos estos sentidos posibles de la palabra 'fantasma', resulta llamativo la recurrencia que se observa en ellos del concepto de 'imagen' o de 'representación': 'objeto impreso en la fantasía', 'visión quimérica', 'imagen de aquel que vuelve de entre los muertos', persona que pretende ser otro por envanecida y presuntuosa, posibilidad de un riesgo futuro o de que algo vacío y sin vida ocupe un espacio. Todas estas reiteraciones enunciadas en torno a la conflictiva relación entre 'presencia' y 'ausencia' constituyen, por otra parte y tal y como explicó José Ricardo Morales en su extraordinaria *Mímesis dramática* (1992), los elementos fundamentales sobre los que se levanta el hecho teatral. ¿Qué es un actor sobre el escenario sino un espectro, una presencia condenada a desaparecer que tan sólo se hace visible durante un lapso de tiempo determinado ante los espectadores? ¿Qué es una obra teatral sino una aparición de fantasmas, de entidades que tan sólo se corporeizan en el específico momento de su representación? ¿Qué es un texto teatral sino una 'población no habitada' en la que cada personaje, cada situación y cada parlamento son elementos impresos en la fantasía, encarnados por personas disfrazadas cuyos conflictos individuales y colectivos se nutren de 'amenazas', 'riesgos' y 'temores'? Y, llevando este planteamiento a un plano superior, si aceptamos que la realidad es discursiva o, como afirma Morales, que nuestro mundo es un 'alucinante teatro de sombras', ¿qué es la Historia sino un sujeto espectral sin motor ni fines? Aquí *Ligazón*, los 'espectros' de Marx y las 'fantasmagorías' de Morales se dan la mano.

Por tanto, cabe preguntarse para cerrar esta reflexión inicial, ¿qué es una 'fantasmagoría'? El término proviene del francés 'fantasmagorie' y según el Diccionario de la Real Academia tiene dos posibles acepciones: '1. Arte de representar figuras por medio de una ilusión óptica; y 2. Ilusión de los sentidos o figuración vana de la inteligencia, desprovista de todo fundamento'. Como se puede apreciar aquí, el concepto de 'fantasmagoría' ofrece una doble dimensión que enriquece nuestra lectura de las obras de Morales. El teatro podría acogerse fácilmente a esa definición de 'Arte de representar figuras' y también a la de 'Ilusión de los sentidos', de la misma manera que la vida, no sólo dentro de la metáfora de 'El Gran

Teatro del Mundo' calderoniana, se articula como una realidad discursiva.

Como ya nos explicaba Esther Peeren en *The Spectral Metaphor* (2014), la metáfora del espectro como posibilidad de hacer visible lo invisible es un elemento recurrente en la literatura y el arte modernos. En nuestra opinión, incluso podríamos afirmar que se trata de uno de los constituyentes esenciales de cualquier representación teatral: el escenario vacío está poblado de apariciones durante el montaje. Cada 'aparición' es única porque cada puesta en escena es siempre irrepetible y perecedera. Por todo ello, la espectralidad del teatro es la de una presencia que regresa cada día a la escena para desaparecer en seguida dejando su impronta en el pensamiento del espectador, en una suerte de anticipación reflexiva que desborda los límites temporales y espaciales del escenario. En este sentido, tenemos la tendencia a relacionar erróneamente al espectro con elementos que regresan del pasado sin darnos cuenta, en muchas ocasiones, de que lo espectral nos anticipa un mundo que aún tiene que tomar forma, que aún está por corporeizarse y, consecuentemente, sobre el que aún tenemos la posibilidad de intervenir. He aquí, desde nuestra perspectiva, uno de los principios fundamentales de un volumen como *Fantasmagorías* de José Ricardo Morales. En sus páginas el espectro no es sólo una metáfora de una condena o de un pasado que se hace presente, sino también de un porvenir aún por definir y que podemos, por ende, anticipar. Así lo entiende el propio Morales cuando afirma en el prólogo:

> Con tales motivos, las cuatro piezas que este libro acoge manifiestan aspectos del alucinante teatro de sombras que constituye nuestro mundo, aquí sujeto a un análisis espectral —¿qué otro le cabe?—, y puesto en pie sobre una escena de apariciones, en la que surgen y se esfuman fugaces fantasmas dramáticos,

> acompañados de su correspondiente corte o cohorte de fantasmones y fantoches (Morales, 1981:11).

De este modo el análisis espectral, ya indicado por Morales con las palabras anteriores, queda plenamente justificado ante las obras de *Fantasmagorías*. Obras que, además, Morales revisita tras años de su primera escritura, convertidos así también estos textos en fantasmas que, ante el intento de rescritura por parte de nuestro autor, se le escapan en versiones sucesivas:

> El escritor, como suelen decir del criminal, vuelve siempre "al lugar del crimen". Y en semejante reiteración encuentra su castigo. Pues por más vueltas que le dé a la obra —imaginándola— y aunque regrese sobre ella con obsesiva asiduidad —pergeñándola—, sus intentos habrán de parecerle vanos. Porque cualquier versión que el autor nos proponga de su idea, no es sino un paso hacia un horizonte que se le aleja con el paso que dio. Este libro da patencia muy clara de la imposibilidad que experimenta el autor cuando pretende definir su conjetura inicial: un espectro evasivo, tan inasible que al adquirir forma propia se pierde con ella. En testimonio de dicha dificultad, el libro se compone de segundas versiones, que, para el escritor, nunca fueron buenas, porque nunca las hallará definitivas. A lo sumo, y con respecto de las precedentes, quizá las considere algo más definidas. Tales versiones se hacen presentes como fantasmagorías o apariciones dotadas de palabra (Morales, 1981:11).

Por tanto, en este volumen de 1981 nos encontramos con versiones de cuatro obras escritas anteriormente: *Hay una nube en su futuro* (1965); *La Imagen* (1975); *Las horas contadas* (1967) y *Oficio de tinieblas* (1966). A estas obras las acompaña un prólogo de José Ricardo Morales en el que, además de realizar las precisiones ya estudiadas sobre los conceptos de espectro y de espectralidad, nuestro dramaturgo aporta unas breves líneas esenciales sobre el proceso de escritura de las piezas y el conflicto esencial que cada una de ellas plantean y desarrollan.

Los cambios que suponen las diferencias entre unas versiones y otras son dignas de una edición crítica de los textos de *Fantasmagorías*, lo cual desborda el presente marco de este trabajo. Sin embargo he creído interesante apuntarlo, ya que un estudio de los procesos de escritura de las obras podría arrojar una visión complementaria a la que aquí, a continuación, ofrecemos en el marco de la espectralidad.

***Hay una nube en su futuro* (1965)**

Efectivamente, *Fantasmagorías* constituye un volumen de verdaderas reescrituras, tal y como Pérez afirmaba en la noticia publicada en *Las últimas noticias*. En esas líneas leíamos que 'El volumen reúne "segundas versiones", verdaderas reescrituras (…)'. De *Hay una nube en su futuro* se nos informaba en esa nota de prensa que 'surgió como presagio de calamidades ecológicas entonces futuras, y que pertenecen hoy a nuestro presente más inmediato. La pieza logra efectos de fábula alucinante, al retomar el mito de Prometeo, a quien se le devuelve el fuego, poderosa fuerza creadora que en manos del hombre se convierte en una grotesca fábrica de humo' (Pérez, 1981:7). Para Morales, esta obra indaga en torno a lo siguiente:

> El exterminio general, puesto graciosamente al alcance de todos los humanos y provocado mediante el uso irracional e inmoral de la técnica presente, es uno de los motivos capitales de *Hay una nube en su futuro*, 1965, cuyo segundo acto, tal y como aquí aparece, difiere substancialmente del original que vio la luz en

> Chile y en España. La obra se concibió como anuncio posible de daños y desastres ambientales que ahora nos agobian, dándonos, además, presentimiento de la otra catástrofe mayor, la nuclear, amenazante y al acecho en la próxima esquina de los tiempos (Morales, 1981:10).

Si bien *Hay una nube en su futuro* es una exploración sobre la posibilidad de una gran catástrofe, la reflexión de Morales desborda lo anecdótico para llevarnos a un conflicto de mayor entidad. En otros trabajos hemos insistido en que uno de los pilares sobre los que se asienta el teatro de Morales es el concepto de 'tecnolatría'. Para Morales nuestro mundo moderno ha operado una sustitución del objeto sobre el que se construye la fe religiosa al desplazar el 'Theo' (es decir, Dios) por el "Techno" o, en otras palabras, por la Tecnificación. Por su parte, el concepto de 'Idolatría' remite a una adoración indebida de los ídolos. Según la Iglesia Católica una persona comete 'idolatría' cuando, en lugar de a Dios, venera y reverencia a una criatura, ya se refiera a dioses, demonios, raza, ancestros, Estado, dinero o poder, por mencionar algunas de sus figuras a modo de ejemplo. Así pues Morales, ya en *Hay una nube en su futuro,* acierta a comprender este mecanismo de sustitución y de desplazamiento. Por eso nos alerta ante el proceso intelectual por el que se construye una religión de la tecnificación y del que, en este 'anuncio dramático', ya nos previene sobre los peligros de la energía nuclear anticipando un desastre de enormes consecuencias como fue el de Chernóbil. En este sentido, es preciso recordar una entrevista publicada en la página 15 de *El Mercurio,* el 1 de julio de 1990, donde Morales explicaba que:

> Ahora se habla mucho de tecnología, pero esa tecnología implica técnica, o sea, "disposición productiva", como dice Aristóteles, y agrega: "acompañada de ra-

> zón verdadera”. La técnica no es tecnología si no tiene un pensamiento que la legitime, y ese pensamiento está fuera de la técnica, está sobre ella. Pensamos sobre las cosas. Los griegos Platón y Aristóteles, cuando proponen la técnica, lo hacen como tecnología. Hoy hablamos mucho de tecnología, pero tenemos una técnica sin “logos”. Ese es el problema, porque el “logos” es precisamente el razonamiento o fundamentación exclusivamente humano o humanístico (Quintana, 1990:15).

En la misma dirección de estas reflexiones, Morales dictó una memorable conferencia en la clausura del Congreso Internacional, *Valencia, Capital Cultural de la República 1936-1937,* que fue editada por la Universidad de Valencia en 1998. El título de esa conferencia es ‘De las ideolatrías a la tecnolatría’ y la podemos encontrar también publicada en 2012 en el segundo volumen de las *Obras Completas* correspondiente a los *Ensayos*, edición a cargo de Manuel Aznar Soler, por la Fundación Alfons el Magnànim. Morales explica ahí que el irracionalismo de la tecnificación carece de ‘logos’, es decir, de la imprescindible reflexión humana que la desacralice. Por tanto, en un contexto de progresiva globalización en el que la técnica se convierte en objeto de adoración, la capacidad de razonar va siendo expulsada hacia la periferia, hacia lo marginal.

En *Hay una nube en su futuro*, Prometeo, el inventor, entrega a los hombres la tecnología nuclear que los lleva a su propia destrucción. La estructura de la obra contiene un juego de espejos, ya que los personajes afirman leer el libreto de una ópera escrita por un tal Morales, cuyo texto se desarrolla a lo largo de toda la pieza dramática. Los personajes se leen como personajes escritos por un Morales que comparte con José Ricardo Morales el marchamo de no provenir ni de “Senegal ni de Oxford”. Con fina ironía se reclama así algo que también encontramos en las propias declaraciones de nuestro autor que, en diversas ocasiones, ha explicado que las modas literarias y artísticas han obstaculizado la incorporación de sus textos a los circuitos profesionales de la escena teatral.

Así pues y sin duda, Morales nos propone un juego textual, pero al mismo tiempo que nos invita a esbozar una sonrisa nos proporciona un conjunto de claves sobre las que se asienta una sólida posición de denuncia no sólo de la fe ciega en lo técnico, sino también de la corrupción política y de lo absurdo de un mundo, el nuestro, en el que los resultados comerciales usurpan toda voluntad de raciocinio. Morales ha declarado al respecto que:

> Como era de esperar, esta pieza tuvo el destino común a las anticipaciones, consistente en que no se les presta la menor atención antes de que se cumplan; después, si es que suceden, se olvidan los presagios y se atiende a los hechos, con descuido absoluto de los motivos que los originaron. Por ello, sería deseable que ciertos ecólogos, al remitirse a los efectos pavorosos de nuestras técnica, de su potencia y sus residuos mortales, y a la par que analizan algunas condiciones negativas de la vida presente, dándonos, para contrarrestarlas, los consabidos consejos del abuelito —"no fumad, no derrochéis, no hagáis ruido…"—, debieran de reflexionar, además, sobre la condición del hombre —en cuanto artificializador o desnaturalizador y técnico—, para desarrollar un pensamiento que fundamentara y concediera auténtico sentido a sus consideraciones utilitarias, meramente instrumentales y, por ello, malamente técnicas. Sin embargo, si procedieran de este modo, podrá decirse que en vez de ecólogos oficiarían de filósofos, y esa especie, como muy bien sabemos, está casi extinguida… por razones técnicas. También lo está la de los dramaturgos, por motivos análogos. Pero,

> al menos, estas y otras inconsecuencias pueden servirnos para sobrevivir en el oficio, llevándolas a escena (Morales, 1981:10).

Más allá de la ironía que destila el texto anterior, constatamos una reflexión que atraviesa todo el volumen de *Fantasmagorías* y que se encuentra especialmente bien definida en *Hay una nube en su futuro*: el pensamiento utilitario anula la condición del hombre. Llevada al extremo, esta idea tiene un efecto paradójico porque, aunque invita a la risa, convoca al espectador a meditar sobre este asunto a la vez que alimenta su espíritu crítico. Cuando escuchamos el parlamento del Ministro en la página 56 del primer volumen de las *Obras Completas*, no estamos tan sólo ante el efecto cómico de lo que podría parecer una caricatura, sino que su autenticidad dramática en seguida evoca en el espectador la analogía con la realidad política que conoce:

> Ministro. *(Usa el micrófono del traje).* —Amado pueblo: para felicidad de todos, concentraremos fuego vivo en cápsulas. Y en previsión de daños y perjuicios, devolveremos de una vez todo el fuego a los dioses, sus autores. Por la justicia y por la paz perpetua, ¡todo el fuego a los dioses!

El espectro del Ministro, en su dimensión fantasmagórica, evoca otro fantasma, éste ya perfectamente conocido en nuestro mundo moderno, como es el de la hecatombe nuclear. Por tanto, aquí, la 'fantasmagoría' se desenvuelve en un espacio triple: el del advenimiento de una catástrofe, el de la impostura y el de la ilusión literaria. De esta manera, la espectralidad de *Hay una nube en su futuro* visibiliza y da cuerpo a una concepción naturalizada de la 'tecnología' como 'tecnolatría'. Morales, al hacer visible el absurdo moral e ideológico sobre el que se asienta la religión de la tecnificación, 'espectraliza' una idea en la escena, de tal manera que el espectador no tiene otra opción que no sea la de confrontarla con su propio esquema mental de pensamiento.

Las horas contadas

En la versión de *Las horas contadas* incluida en *Fantasmagorías*, encontramos otro de los temas presentes en las obras de José Ricardo Morales: el tiempo habitado. Morales afirma en el prólogo que en esta pieza 'se aborda el tema del tiempo que matamos y nos mata —en *Las horas contadas*, 1967, ahora escrita de nuevo íntegramente—' (Morales, 1981:11). Por su parte, Floridor Pérez añadía en su ya mencionada nota de *Las Últimas Noticias* que esta obra constituye 'un monólogo que aborda el implacable paso del tiempo que tratamos de matar mientras nos mata. La reelaboración, en este caso, apunta a cierta depuración del lenguaje escénico, eliminando efectos de sospechoso gusto' (Pérez, 1981:7).

En realidad, bien podríamos definir este monólogo como una aparición. El personaje de la mujer 'se presenta en escena cuando el público inicie las naturales protestas', nos indica una acotación inicial. Además el recurso del teatro dentro del teatro como espacio de posibilidades dramatúrgicas también está presente al comienzo de esta obra. La mujer declara ir 'al teatro. Eso de *Las horas contadas* promete. Y aquí me tienen viendo el espectáculo: una sala con gente'. Este cambio de perspectiva por el que los espectadores se convierten en el elenco de personajes y la mujer en espectadora, produce un efecto de incertidumbre en el público. De ahí que la mujer prosiga afirmando que 'Lo gracioso, y por eso me reía, es que a mí, como espectadora, me pagan, y a ustedes, como actores, no sólo no les pagan sino que les cobran'. Se trata del fantasma de Scheherazada. En el teatro, en la verdad de la escena, el fantasma deviene en una entidad corporea al 'contarle' las horas al público. De este modo, leemos hacia el final del monólogo lo siguiente:

> Sin explicarse cómo, contemplaba una escena fantástica, situada en algo así como un teatro imaginario. Desde la sombra de la higuera descubrió a Scheherazada en una triste habitación de color amarillo. Vestía un traje astroso y sucio. Y la encontró vieja y cansada, sin lecho ni mesa, con una sola silla, sola (Morales, 1981:70).

La figura de Scherezade más consolidada en nuestro imaginario común es la de una mujer joven que cuenta historias para salvar su vida; sin embargo aquí se nos presenta a una mujer mayor, casi una vagabunda, protagonista principal de un teatro imaginario pero al que en realidad están asistiendo los espectadores en este juego metateatral. Se nos cuenta que esta mujer:

> Tenía por oficio imaginar un largo sueño ante varios actores que se desempeñaban como espectadores, en el que el tiempo no quedaba ni pasaba, en el que nadie vivía ni moría, y en el que se contaban sólo horas: las horas y minutos y segundos de aquellos que buscaban pasatiempo, para olvidar en éste la rueda de los años y los días, con sus horas, minutos y segundos… Los actores, puestos ante sí mismos, asistían a esa escena inquietante, suspendidos en el tiempo inventado por el espectador único (70).

De la cita anterior es necesario destacar esta idea del 'espectador único' donde actores y espectadores son otros y sí mismos a un tiempo. Como si se tratara de una imagen creada por el pintor M.C.Escher en la que unas manos se pintan a sí mismas emergiendo del dibujo, los actores y los espectadores conforman una especie de 'Aleph'. Actores y espectadores emergen como un espectro. La única brecha en este círculo 'real o imaginario' se encuentra en el concepto mismo de verosimilitud y en el grado en que el espectador esté dispuesto a aceptarlo o no como esencia de lo teatral. Por ello, el monólogo prosigue con las siguientes palabras:

> Hasta que alguno de ellos, quizá para romper el círculo real o imaginario, exclamó con violencia: "¡Inverosímil! ¡Falso! ¡Eso nunca sucede!". ¿Inverosímil? ¿Falso? ¿Quién dijo semejante cosa? Entonces, ¿qué ha ocurrido aquí? ¿Nada? ¿Cómo se atreven a suponerlo? ¿No se trataba de matar el tiempo? ¿No les hice pasar largos minutos sin sentirlo? ¿Qué más quieren? No engañamos a nadie. Nuestro espectáculo es el único absolutamente verdadero. No hay ninguno más cierto, pueden estar seguros. ¿Es que no tienen todos las horas contadas? Entonces, desde la sombra de la higuera, vio cómo Scheherazada, dirigiéndose al público, decía: "Inverosímil. Falso. Estoy de acuerdo. Sigan ustedes. Sigan. Aquí tienen mi asiento. Le cedo el turno a otro. Que nos cuente su sueño, a ver si puede". Y Scheherazada, sin añadir palabra, se levantó y salió (Morales, 1981:71).

Por tanto, el espectador se convierte en actor de su propia obra y en el discurrir de ese viaje tan sólo hay un principio de verdad que mantiene constante su pulso: el paso del tiempo. Juega Morales aquí con la polisemia del término 'contadas', que por un lado es sinónimo de 'narradas' y por otro de 'enumeradas' en su sentido aritmético. Ambos significados confluyen en una noción última de tiempo y de finitud que tan sólo puede superar el espectro del actor corporeizado una y otra vez, siempre igual, siempre distinto, en el imaginario del espectador. El teatro es una fantasmagoría, parece que nos dice Morales, en su sentido de ilusión óptica y de desbordamiento de los límites temporales. No hay nada más auténtico ni más real, podríamos concluir, que la espectralidad porque es lo único que no está sujeto a la finitud del tiempo.

La imagen

Como hemos advertido en otros trabajos, los subtítulos de las piezas dramáticas de Morales son sumamente importantes porque siempre nos indican y proponen una dirección de lectura. El de esta obra es 'Fantasmagoría en dos actos', no sólo orienta sino que ya explicita el carácter que le concede el autor. El texto dramático se sitúa temporalmente en el siglo XIII. Si recordamos una de las acepciones del concepto de fantasma que ya comentamos anteriormente, entre ellas se encontraba el de 'espantajo'. En la acotación inicial del primer acto leemos: 'Su Excelencia, espantajo de paja, cuero, trapo y madera carcomida, está sentado en el trono, sobre un estrado, frente a los espectadores' (Morales, 1981: 73). Efectivamente, nos encontramos ya inicialmente con que su Excelencia es un espectro, una imagen por definición. La crítica al poder absoluto que proseguirá queda nítidamente enmarcada por la maestría de Morales.

El espectro del poder es una presencia incorpórea entre los cortesanos. Todos ellos se preguntan por la salud de su Excelencia, pero en realidad a nadie le interesa su estado físico sino su imagen, porque salud e imagen, realidad y distorsión, se establecen como verdad sin distinción:

> Doña Sol.— Por cierto, ya lo dije. Pero esos rumores que no existen, aluden a la salud de Su Excelencia.
> Don García. —Seamos precisos. ¿A qué se refieren? ¿A Su Excelencia o a su imagen? ¿A la salud de Su Excelencia o a la de su imagen? ¿A la imagen de la salud de Su Excelencia o a la imagen de la salud de su imagen?
> Doña Sol. —A todos esos puntos. ¿Y qué diagnóstico establece?

> Don García. —En casa caso es diferente... Pero en todos resultará idéntico (Morales, 1981: 78).

Su Excelencia, un espectro sin voluntad, deja el gobierno en manos de su corte, que regula metódica y absurdamente cada aspecto de la vida. Como en un momento determinado expondrán Doña Ana y Doña Clavel, su Excelencia no está ni vivo ni muerto, a lo que esta última añadirá: 'Sí, sí... Conozco la frase oficial: "Su imagen perdurará eternamente en nuestro corazones...". Esta última frase es tan 'oficial' como que fue utilizada por la propaganda del régimen de Pinochet. En este sentido, llama la atención que la censura de entonces en Chile, —no debemos olvidar que la obra ya fue escrita en 1975 y vuelta a publicar en 1981—, no percibiera que Morales introducía aquí con fina ironía frases de las que poblaban los discursos oficiales de entonces. La obra nos sitúa ante la descomposición y corrupción que conlleva como esencia cualquier régimen de poder dictatorial y totalitario. En palabras de Pérez, 'Lo que el afán de lucro causa en la naturaleza, acarrea en la sociedad el ansia de poder, como se ve en *La Imagen* (fantasmagoría en dos actos)' (Pérez, 1981: 7). O incluso el propio Morales en el prólogo nos advertía que:

> *La Imagen*, 1975, supone la representación de un régimen inamovible, totalitario, gobierno de la muerte y con la muerte —corrupto, como le pertenece—, un poder que pretende perpetuarse indefinidamente, cualquiera sean las circunstancias, con recurso a los medios sucedáneos y coactivos de que ahora disponen los Estados en cualquier latitud —televisión, consignas, propaganda; imágenes en vez de consistencias, apariencias en lugar de entidades reales—, manipulados sin escrúpulo alguno, para exclusivo beneficio de quienes los emplean. La obra, tal como aparece en estas páginas, acrecentó considerablemente su extensión,

> respecto del texto publicado en Estados Unidos, 1977, incluyéndose en ella varias escenas y pasajes nuevos (Morales, 1981: 10-11).

Para Morales la televisión, la publicidad y la propaganda son medios fantasmagóricos porque convocan una ilusión. En el caso de *La Imagen* se trata de un espejismo con el que se persigue un fin muy concreto: la perpetuación de unas estructuras determinadas de poder. Don Fadrique, tras un golpe de Estado que derroca al gobierno anterior, afirmará que 'aunque la imagen cambia, el hombre es siempre el mismo' (134); a lo que seguirá la lectura de una carta por la que se adjudica poderes absolutos: 'A las nueve horas del día veinticinco de febrero de mil novecientos setenta y cinco, yo don Fadrique, por la Gracia de Dios, ordeno y mando que yo, don Fadrique, por la Gracia de Dios, en estas dolorosas circunstancias cumpla con el deber de hacerse cargo de la nación. Publíquese. Comuníquese' (134-35). La fecha, 1975, contrasta con la indicación inicial en la acotación que situaba toda la escena en una corte medieval del siglo XIII. El efecto de este detalle es enormemente perturbador para el espectador, ya que si la analogía de las acciones, personajes y parlamentos con el régimen dictatorial de Pinochet estaba sutilmente señalada, la fecha destaca la radical actualidad de la denuncia que supone esta obra en el contexto chileno del momento.

Morales, anticipa así el concepto de espectralidad enunciado por Derrida, cuya intuición ya estaba en el *Manifiesto Comunista* de Marx y Engels. Muestra y desmantela en escena los principios constituyentes del poder espectral del totalitarismo. Fadrique construye su 'imagen' y desde ella el poder se consolida y perpetúa gracias a su dimensión fantasmagórica.

Oficio de tinieblas

Sobre *Oficio de tinieblas* hemos publicado recientemente un trabajo en las páginas de la revista *Primer Acto* (2013) al que remitimos al lector ya que nuestro análisis de la obra no sería más que una repetición de lo que en esa ocasión expusimos. Aún así consideramos que, al hilo del concepto de espectralidad que estamos analizando para la totalidad del volumen de *Fantasmagorías*, es necesario aportar aquí algunas notas complementarias.

En el prólogo de *Fantasmagorías*, Morales expone que 'la ocasión patética de la muerte personal aparece en *Oficio de tinieblas*, 1966 —reducida a su mínima expresión, si se compara con sus primeras ediciones chilena y española—, obra que representa nuestra vida como un oscuro, incierto menester, y en un desolador misterio profano' (Morales, 1981: 11). Por su lado, Pérez comentaba que:

> La pieza final, *Oficio de Tinieblas*, dramatiza la muerte propia, y representa nuestra vida como 'un oscuro, incierto menester'. En general, el hombre resulta el personaje de su propia obra, y como tal, debe ceñirse al 'libreto', cuyo desenlace va conociendo sólo a medida que actúa (vive). La gran incógnita es ¿cuánto falta para que caiga el telón? (Pérez, 1981: 7).

Desde luego, esta última obra representa nuestra vida como un deambular de espectros en el seno de una insondable oscuridad. Concordamos con Morales cuando afirma que se trata de un 'desolador misterio profano'. Al mismo tiempo pensamos, puesta ya la obra en perspectiva y tras el estudio que le dedicamos en las páginas de *Primer Acto*, que además en el volumen *Fantasmagorías* adquiere un sentido añadido de cierre del análisis espectral al que Morales somete a nuestro mundo. Ese sentido adicional radica en el diálogo que *Oficio de tinieblas* mantiene con *Ligazón. Auto para siluetas* de Ramón María del Valle-Inclán. Si en *Ligazón* ya adivinaba Valle-Inclán las posibilidades que podría brindar un teatro de sombras, Morales realiza una apuesta mucho más valiente y radical al atreverse a plantear una pieza dramática que se desarrolla en la absoluta oscuridad de un teatro y que tan sólo cuente con las voces de los actores. Aquí Morales alcanza el efecto de plena espectralidad al conseguir que las voces de los actores adquieran corporeidad en la imaginación de los espectadores mediante el único instrumento de la palabra.

Conclusiones

En su artículo de *Las Últimas Noticias*, Floridor Pérez explicaba que 'todo dramaturgo crea para ser visto en una sala, pero la elaborada perfección formal del texto de Morales, siempre atento a utilizar la máxima función poética del lenguaje, hace de *Fantasmagorías* teatro apto para leerse y meditarse. Para representarse en la interioridad de un lector, que no puede negar su condición de personaje' (Pérez, 1981:7). Sin duda, el lector no puede negar su condición de personaje y además, añadimos, de espectro. Todo personaje se construye como imagen y toda imagen es siempre un espectro. Morales ha sufrido durante demasiados años un 'destiempo' que, por otra parte, es una de las claves configuradoras de su producción dramática y de toda la literatura producida en el destierro. Morales, en una entrevista concedida a Sonia Quintana en el año 1991 y publicada en las páginas de *El Mercurio*, explicaba que la diferencia entre la fama y el prestigio por un lado, frente al reconocimiento por otro, estriba en el hecho de que 'reconocer' es conocer a alguien en profundidad.

En ese sentido, el análisis espectral que José Ricardo Morales propone en las páginas de *Fantasmagorías* no ha tenido, en nuestra opinión, el 'reconocimiento' que se merece debido en buena parte a la carencia de traducciones que poseemos de los textos de Morales a otras lenguas, aparte de la insuficiencia de los estudios en la propia. De lo contrario, probablemente el giro espectral de Derrida y la constitución de los estudios sobre el concepto de espectralidad no se hubiera centrado tanto en la metáfora del espectro como fantasma que vuelve del pasado, como símbolo del poder o como agente de intervención en el ámbito público que hace visible lo invisible. Paradójicamente, aunque anterior, la propuesta explícita y su visión en los textos teatrales de Morales es infinitamente más rica y compleja. Para Morales la espectralidad no sólo es una categoría historiográfica que nos advierte de cómo el fenómeno del destierro se asienta en un permanente destiempo o es una metáfora que integra todo un conjunto de símbolos de la marginalidad que se vuelven visibles, sino que constituye, por encima de todo, una estrategia de pensamiento que desnaturaliza todo aquello que nuestros esquemas mentales asumen como natural y verdadero.

Por tanto, en *Fantasmagorías,* lo espectral no es adjetivo o ni siquiera una metáfora, sino una modalidad de reflexión y de análisis que comienza donde termina la rigidez de un sistema de representación del mundo dominante y asentado en oposiciones dicotómicas de elementos contrarios. En conclusión, para Morales, tal y como propone en este volumen, el mundo es un alucinante teatro de espectros donde el otro puede ser el mismo, donde lo invisible es visible, donde el actor y el espectador son distintos y uno al mismo tiempo.

Obras Citadas

Ahumada, H. (2000). 'José Ricardo Morales «a la intemperie»'. *Signos*. XXIII (segundo semestre). 48. 3-12.

____. (2002). 'Viajero esencial José Ricardo Morales y su teatro del exilio'. *Acotaciones*. 9 (julio-diciembre). 45-63.

____. y Godoy Gallardo, E. (2002). 'Un dramaturgo al trasluz, José Ricardo Morales y su teatro del exilio'. *Revista Chilena de Literatura*. (Abril). 60. 125-137.

Arévalo Cortés, J. (1992). 'El sinsentido del mundo: Teatro de una pieza (1965), de José Ricardo Morales'. *Anthropos*. 133 (junio). 65-73.

Aznar Soler, M. ed. (1992a). *José Ricardo Morales, Un dramaturgo del destierro. Creación dramática y pensamiento crítico. Anthropos*, 133 (junio). número monográfico.

____. (1992b). 'El teatro de José Ricardo Morales'. *Anthropos* 133 (junio). 32-37.

Castedo-Ellerman, E. (1982). 'José Ricardo Morales'. *El teatro chileno de mediados de siglo*. Santiago de Chile: Editorial Andrés Bello. 141-163.

____. (1992). 'Un dramaturgo que valora la palabra: José Ricardo Morales'. *Anthropos*. 133 (junio). 47-49.

Derrida, J. (1993) *Spectres de Marx*. Paris: Galilée.

Doménech, R. (1977). 'Aproximación al teatro del exilio' en AAVV, *El exilio español de 1939 Tomo IV (Cultura y literatura)*. José Luis Abellán (ed.). Madrid: Taurus. 189; 190; 229-231; 235-237; 243; 244.

____. (2006). 'José Ricardo Morales' en 'Introducción' a *Teatro del exilio: obras en un acto*. Madrid: Fundamentos. 38-45.

____. (2013). *El teatro del exilio*. Madrid: Cátedra.

Godoy Gallardo, E. (2000). 'El teatro de José Ricardo Morales' en prólogo a *Teatro* de José Ricardo Morales. Santiago de Chile: Universidad Andrés Bello. 7-30.

____. (2001). 'Teoría y práctica de las *Españoladas* en el teatro de José Ricardo Morales'. *Revista Signos* XXXIV. 49-50. 21-33.

____. (2003). 'La trayectoria de todo un dramaturgo'. *Primer Acto*. 298 (abril-mayo-junio). 28-35 (entrevista).

____. (2007). 'Tres miradas sobre Don Juan desde el exilio: Ramón Sender, José Ricardo Morales y Salvador de Madariaga'. *Mapocho*. 62 (segundo semestre). 1-23.

Marx, K. y Engels, F. (1848). *Manifest der Kommunistischen Partei*. Londres.

Monleón, J. (1969). 'Morales, un español en la inmensa ninguna parte' en *Teatro*. Madrid: Taurus. Colección El Mirlo Blanco. 9-28.

____. (1970). 'Encuentro tardío y necesario con el exiliado José Ricardo Morales'. *Primer Acto*. 122 (julio). 42-49; reproducido en *Españoladas* de José Ricardo Morales. Madrid: Fundamentos, 1987. 132-142.

____. (1973). 'Con José Ricardo Morales, peregrino en su patria y autor de ninguna parte', *Triunfo*. 563 (julio), 34-36 (entrevista).

____. (1992). 'Max Aub y José Ricardo Morales, dos dramaturgos de la España marginal', *Anthropos*. 133 (junio). 60-62.

Morales, J. R. (1981). *Fantasmagorías*. Santiago de Chile: Editorial Universitaria.

____. (1992). *Mímesis Dramática*. Santiago de Chile – Madrid: Editorial Universitaria y Primer Acto.

____. (2012). *Obras Completas: Ensayos*. Edición a cargo de Manuel Aznar Soler. Valencia: Alfons el Magnànim.

Peeren, E. y Blanco, M. P. *The Spectralities Reader: Ghosts and Haunting in Contemporary Cultural Theory*. Londres: Bloombsury. 2013.

____. (2014). *The spectral metaphor. Living ghosts and the Agency of Invisibility*. New York: Palgrave Macmillan.

Pérez, F. (2-8-1981). '¿Fantasmagorías?' en *Las Últimas Noticias*.7.

Quintana, S. (1-7-1990). 'El hombre en su esencialidad no cambia' en *El Mercurio*. 15.

Valdivia, P. (2011). 'José Ricardo Morales: el exilio interminable'. *El Genio Maligno: Revista de Humanidades y Ciencias Sociales*. 9. 72-89.

____. (2013a). '*Poetas en el destierro* de José Ricardo Morales: un editor entre dos mundos'. *Mapocho*. 74. 129-146

____. (2013b). 'Tres piezas dramáticas en un acto de José Ricardo Morales: *Oficio de tinieblas*, *La corrupción al alcance de todos* y *Sobre algunas especies en vías de extinción*. *Primer Acto*. 345. 2.

____. (2013c). '*Ardor con ardor se apaga* de José Ricardo Morales y la actualización de la noción de 'las tres culturas' como estrategia discursiva'. *Dialogía*. 7. 174-195.

____. (2014). 'José Ricardo Morales a tiempo: algunas claves de lectura de su obra dramática'. *Puentes*. 2.

Valdivia Milla, B. y Galeote, M. (2010), 'Vivir como extranjero: a propósito de José Ricardo Morales Malva'. Granada: Junta de Andalucía, Biblioteca Virtual de Andalucía.

9. La habitación de Carrasco: el espectro a la intemperie

Intemperie de Jesús Carrasco ha conocido una importante campaña de promoción que hasta ahora no se había producido con ningún otro autor en la literatura española reciente. La novela apareció a comienzos de 2013 publicándose de manera simultánea en distintos países. Diversos críticos intentaron, durante todo el año 2013, adscribir esta novela a un conjunto de referentes conocidos por el público lector (Azancot, 4-2-2013; Fontana, 19-1-2013; González Peón, 4-2-2013; López Palacios, 1-2-2013; Medina Díaz, 6-5-2013; Niño, 26-5-2013; Pozuelo Yvancos, 19-1-2013; Sanz Villanueva, 2013; Senabre, 18-1-2013). Esta ansiedad por 'ubicar' la novela de Jesús Carrasco ha llevado a la construcción de una cierta genealogía literaria de ese texto en relación con obras de Miguel Delibes, Coetzee, William Faulkner (*As I lay dying*) y de Cormac McCarthy (*On the road*) que, si en algunos casos ha encontrado cierta hospitalidad en las declaraciones públicas del propio autor (López Iturriaga, 5-8-2013), no siempre ha enriquecido la lectura del texto sino que la ha encorsetado dentro de un espacio de las supuestas influencias: un campo siempre goloso para el crítico pero a veces reducido a una mecanicista de transfusión de temas y de estilos de unos autores a otros.

En las próximas páginas, sin ánimo de cerrar el texto de la novela a un significado unívoco ni tampoco de caer en el mero determinismo, ofreceré un análisis de *Intemperie* que aporte una construcción complementaria del sentido de esta novela frente a la que se ha establecido en la inmediata recepción de la obra y de la que a continuación procederé a un detenido estudio por mi parte en conexión con el concepto de 'metáfora espectral' propuesto por Esther Peeren en uno de sus últimos estudios: *The spectral metaphor: living ghosts and the Agency of Invisibility* (Peeren, 2014).

El corpus que he seleccionado para este trabajo ocupa el arco cronológico que se levanta desde una de las primeras noticias que surgen sobre *Intemperie* en las páginas de los periódicos del grupo editorial Prensa Ibérica el sábado 13 de octubre de 2012 hasta la elección por los lectores de *El País* como la mejor novela de 2013 el 18 de diciembre de este año. Los medios consultados son los periódicos de principal referencia en España por la larga tradición de sus suplementos culturales: *El País*. *El Mundo* y *ABC*; además de otro tipo de publicaciones como la conocida *Revista Mercurio*, el grupo editorial Prensa Ibérica y la nota oficial de la editorial *Seix Barral* que se hizo llegar a diferentes medios de comunicación a través de la agencia de noticias *Europa Press*. Quedan, por tanto, fuera de este estudio reseñas y noticias que hubieran podido aparecer en medios de menor repercusión por el número de lectores que acuden a sus páginas y otros canales digitales: grupos de lectura online y blogs particulares. Mi perspectiva en la elección de las noticias que voy a estudiar no es tanto exhaustiva sino representativa de una determinada lectura que se configura de la novela en el momento inmediato de su aparición.

El 13 de octubre de 2012, el grupo editorial Prensa Ibérica publicaba en sus páginas de cultura la siguiente noticia 'Jesús Carrasco, el escritor desconocido que está triunfando en Fráncfort'. La nota no venía firmada sino que provenía de la agencia de noticias EFE. Surgió en periódicos de este grupo editorial como el de *La Opinión de Málaga* donde se anuncia ya la aparición de *Intemperie* para enero de 2013 y en la que se destaca el hecho de que su autor, Jesús Carrasco, fuera un autor que anteriormente no hubiera publicado ninguna novela. En palabras del periódico:

> El escritor español Jesús Carrasco, cuya primera novela aparecerá en enero en España en la editorial Seix Barral bajo el título de Intemperie, se ha convertido en

> un autor muy demandado en la Feria del Libro de Fráncfort y su obra ha sido vendida a 13 idiomas extranjeros. La directora de Seix-Barral, Elena Ramírez, explicó que lo que está ocurriendo con Carrasco es "uno de esos milagros que sólo pueden ocurrir en Fráncfort". El autor, según explicó Ramírez, nacido en Badajoz y residente en Sevilla, tiene cerca de cuarenta años, hasta ahora no había publicado novelas y su manuscrito había llegado a la editorial entre los cientos de manuscritos que llegan todos los meses, sin recomendación de ninguna agencia literaria. "Es el libro más importante que he leído en muchos años", aseguró Ramírez, que quedó tan impactada por el manuscrito que, de cara a la feria, empezó a recomendarlo a editores extranjeros que en muchos casos también se vieron atrapados por él. "Algunos lo han comparado con Faulkner y con Coetzee", dijo la editora (La Opinión de Málaga, 2012).

Efectivamente, como bien se expone en la noticia, la Feria del Libro de Frankfurt de 2012 fue el escaparate perfecto para esta obra de un autor hasta entonces desconocido. En las declaraciones que cita ya el periódico correspondiente a la directora de Seix-Barral, ya aparecen dos nombres que la crítica cultural española va a repetir una y otra vez en sus acercamientos a *Intemperie*: Faulkner y Coetzee. Todavía en este momento temprano, no se especifican qué novelas han influido la de Jesús Carrasco aunque en el caso de Faulkner, como sí veremos más adelante, serán dos a la que aludan los críticos: la ya mencionada *As I lay dying* (1930) y *Light in August* (1932). De manera más o menos inconsciente, ya se comienza a delimitar, desde este momento y en los medios de comunicación, un horizonte de influencias genealógicas que van acompañar a *Intemperie* desde su andadura por las librerías españolas. De alguna manera, ya se construía también una cierta lectura de la novela de Jesús Carrasco como de este modo lo atestigua el propio texto de la noticia de *La Opinión de Málaga* al añadir que:

> La novela tiene sólo tres personajes que son un niño, un pastor que lo protege y un alguacil que los persigue a los dos y tiene, según Ramírez, cierta carga alegórica. "Los personajes representan el mal, el bien y la inocencia", dijo Ramírez (La Opinión de Málaga, 2012).

Uno de los trabajos de cualquier editorial es el dar a conocer los libros que publica y además hacer que el público lector se interese por ese producto. Por tanto, resulta muy llamativo constatar que en el mismo momento en el que el mercado estaba apostando por novelas históricas como *El lector de Julio Verne* (2012) de Almudena Grandes, por autores ya consagrados como Manuel Rivas y su libro *Las voces bajas* (2012) y por literatura enclavada en la utilización concreta de lugares y de personajes claramente reconocibles como *La bibliotecaria de Auschwitz* de Antonio G. Iturbe; y que en cambio, desde Seix-Barral, se promocionara una novela sin referentes anclados en la realidad más inmediata o en los dictámenes de la moda. En este sentido, de nuevo la noticia acota una determinada lectura de la novela sobre la que se nos previene que los personajes representan el mal, el bien y la inocencia: tres elementos universales que, expuestos de esa manera y habiendo sido el lector avisado del cierto carácter alegórico del texto, cierran la novela a una interpretación en clave de lectura 'clásica' sin intentar prestigiar la novela por su relación directa con la actualidad política, social o histórica.
El 21 de diciembre de 2012, *Europa Press* publica una noticia en la que da cuenta de *Intemperie*. De nuevo en esta noticia se destacan los mismos aspectos que veíamos en la primera nota de prensa aunque eso sí ya con una cierta mayor elaboración.

En primer lugar, se incide en el hecho del interés que la novela recibió por parte de lo que se califica en el texto como 'las mejores editoriales extranjeras' y se destaca el dato de que 'se editará en trece países'. Además, se indica que desde la editorial Seix Barral nos informan de que '*Intemperie* aúna la riqueza de Miguel Delibes y la fuerza de Cormac McCarthy fundidas en una voz propia' (Europa Press, 2012). La línea de influencias va conformándose. El problema es que esta indicación de la editorial, apropiada y comprensible por la función que cumple, va a ser la referencia central para el periodismo cultural español desplazando lo que Seix Barral señalaba como 'voz propia' hacia un énfasis cada vez mayor en la influencia de otros autores. En la nota además se precisan algunos aspectos del contenido de la novela:

> El libro narra la huida de un niño a través de un país castigado por la sequía y gobernado por la violencia. Un mundo cerrado, sin nombres ni fechas, en el que la moral ha escapado por el mismo sumidero por el que se ha ido el agua. En ese escenario, el niño, aún no del todo malogrado, tendrá la oportunidad de iniciarse en los dolorosos rudimentos del juicio o, por el contrario, de ejercer para siempre la violencia que ha mamado. A través de arquetipos como el niño, el cabrero o el alguacil, Jesús Carrasco 'construye un relato duro, salpicado de momentos de gran lirismo'. 'Una novela tallada palabra a palabra, donde la presencia de una naturaleza inclemente hilvana toda la historia hasta confundirse con la trama y en la que la dignidad del ser humano brota entre las grietas secas de la tierra con una fuerza inusitada'. Jesús Carrasco nació en Badajoz en 1972 y en 2005 se trasladó a Sevilla, donde reside en la actualidad. Desde 1996 trabaja como redactor publicitario, actividad que compagina con la escritura (Europa Press, 2012)

El contenido del anterior extracto es muy clarificador. A la información ya brindada por Elena Ramírez en la noticia que antecedía a ésta, ahora se le suma un conjunto de claves de lectura importantes. Por un lado se explica cuál es el argumento de la novela aunque, debo precisar, que en ningún momento en *Intemperie* se indica si es un país o una región donde se desarrolla la acción. Lo que sí es cierto es que se trata de un territorio inhóspito y hostil. Además encontramos, entre comillas, algunas afirmaciones interesantes pero que la mala redacción de la noticia no nos indica quién las realiza. Por extensión, entiendo que provienen de la misma editorial Seix-Barral. Estas afirmaciones relacionadas con el estilo de la novela, 'una novela tallada palabra a palabra' en la que la 'naturaleza' se funde con la trama y en la que la 'dignidad del ser humano' es uno de los elementos centrales, proporcionan al crítico y al lector unos valiosos puntos de referencia como así lo refrenda la posterior lectura de *Intemperie*.

En declaraciones posteriores, Jesús Carrasco ha manifestado reiteradamente que esta novela es, sobre todo, una exploración sobre el concepto de 'dignidad'. Esta idea, que nosotros hacemos aquí también nuestra, resulta verdaderamente fértil ya que no reduce *Intemperie* ni a un conjunto de convenciones genéricas ni tampoco a una supuesta genealogía de influencias. Insistimos. Desde mi perspectiva considero más enriquecedor estudiar esta novela por lo que es en sí misma, por sus propios valores literarios en suma, más que por aquellos textos a los que pudiéramos pensar que se asemeja.

El 19 de enero de 2013 aparecen, en la página 10 de esta publicación, una entrevista de Antonio Fontana (que aparecerá también el 22-1-2013 en las páginas del diario *ABC*) y una reseña de Pozuelo Yvancos en las páginas de *El Cultural*. Fontana, con bastante agudeza, realiza las tres preguntas fundamentales que todo lector, ante una novela tan singular como *Intemperie*, se cuestiona:

> Un niño que huye, un alguacil que le sigue los pasos. ¿Por qué sabemos tan pocas cosas: los motivos por los que el niño se ha escapado, los motivos por los que es perseguido? [...] Tampoco hay nombres, solo "el niño", "el cabrero", "el alguacil". [...] ¿Qué es "Intemperie"? ¿Un "western"? (Fontana, 2013: 10)

Carrasco contesta que para él 'La imagen incompleta provoca en el receptor una especie de impulso que tiende a completar lo inacabado. Existe, por tanto, un terreno intermedio entre el texto y el lector en el que este se apropia de lo escrito y, en cierto modo, lo finaliza' (Fontana, 19-01-2013: 10). Además añade sobre los personajes que ha 'optado por eliminar lo reconocible como forma de desenfoque, intentando así que lo sustancial, es decir, las relaciones entre los personajes y de los personajes con lo que les rodea, emerja de la manera más nítida posible'. En otras palabras, Carrasco considera que es la condición universal de los personajes y de las acciones la que ocupa el centro de interés de la narración. Por eso, ante la pregunta de '¿Qué es "Intemperie"?', el escritor contesta que denominar esta obra como un western es 'una de las etiquetas posibles' y 'También podría ser una novela de iniciación, una *road movie* o una tragedia clásica'. Como se observa en la anterior declaración, *Intemperie* es, por encima de todo, una narración que aspira a la conformación de un mundo de referentes y de problemas universales que transciendan la anécdota. Esta idea aquí expresada se refrenda en la respuesta de del propio autor cuando Fontana le pregunta sobre qué inspira la novela y nuestro autor contesta que: '*Intemperie* gira en torno a la idea de dignidad. Un concepto de un altísimo valor ético' (Carrasco, 19-01-2013: 10). En cuanto a las influencias, Fontana destaca la huela de Miguel Delibes y de Cormac McCarthy en *Intemperie*. Carrasco reconoce la presencia de ciertos aspectos presentes en las obras de estos dos autores:

'Me reconozco en los paisajes de Delibes' y 'Lo que me maravilla de McCarthy es su aspecto más poético, incluso a la hora de presentarnos escenas de extrema crudeza'. Es decir, Carrasco manifiesta su hospitalidad a elementos característicos de la narrativa de otros autores, lo que no quiere decir, por otro lado, que *Intemperie* sea un mero epígono de Delibes o de McCarthy. Entre otras cosas porque como el propio autor expone: 'Si el estilo pudiera definirse como la marca personal que el autor le imprime al texto, me gustaría que esa marca fuera, en mi caso, lo más tenue posible. Me gustan los autores, o los músicos, que se ponen al servicio de la obra hasta diluirse en ella y desaparecer' (Carrasco, 19-01-2013: 10). El anhelo, por parte de Carrasco, de alcanzar una escritura de referentes universales en la que el autor se sumerja hasta desaparecer en la narración queda más que patente. Por tanto, reducir *Intemperie* a una genealogía de transfusiones literarias comprobamos que se convierte en un esquema simplificador que nos escamotea posibilidades de lectura.

En el mismo número de *El Cultural*, Pozuelo Yvancos escribió una reseña que titulaba como 'Cara y cruz de Jesús Carrasco'. Para Yvancos, *Intemperie* posee un desequilibrio entre lo que él llama 'los elementos de la historia y su lenguaje'. En palabras de este estudioso, la novela tiene un 'excesivo formalismo': 'al no haberse graduado la brillantez de la prosa y su ensimismamiento autocomplaciente en los extremos naturalistas, casi tremendistas, de su desarrollo' (Pozuelo Yvancos, 19-01-2013: 10). En nuestra opinión tal desequilibrio se encuentra más en los ojos del crítico que en la novela misma. Pozuelo Yvancos no se equivoca al decir que la novela está escrita con 'precisión de orfebre' y es precisamente en esa riqueza de conceptos y de lenguaje donde está el valor diferencial de *Intemperie* frente al conjunto de obras escritas en el mismo contexto cultural del momento. Donde Pozuelo Yvancos ve preciosismo, en mi opinión hay una labor de poda y de refinamiento admirable. El mismo Pozuelo Yvancos así parece reconocerlo cuando en su reseña afirma que 'Desde luego, nadie de su generación escribe hoy como lo hace Jesús Carrasco'. Efectivamente, la novela de Jesús Carrasco destaca de una manera muy acusada en comparación con la general pobreza en la expresión de escritores coetáneos. Quizá desde esa perspectiva pueda parecerle al crítico que la escritura de Carrasco se basa en el alarde estilístico, pero si por el contrario contextualizamos *Intemperie* dentro de un horizonte más amplio podemos fácilmente situar a esta novela a la par de otro texto fundamental de la narrativa española como lo fue en su día *Volverás a región* de Juan Benet.

La reseña de Pozuelo Yvancos, elogiosa pero con reservas, contrasta con la que Ricardo Senabre publicó el 18-01-2013, justo un día antes, también en las páginas de *El Cultural*. Senabre califica *Intemperie* como una 'magnífica novela, que sorprende por su madurez narrativa, por la riqueza y precisión de su lenguaje' (Senabre, 18-01-2013). Senabre también acierta a destacar la atemporalidad de la novela y la universalidad de sus personajes. En cuanto a las infuencias, este estudioso emite un juicio mucho más atemperado que otros críticos ya que señala que 'puede recordar en algunos momentos obras como *Las ratas*, de Delibes, o *La carretera*, de Cormac McCarthy. Conviene subrayar que tales semejanzas son lejanísimas y superficiales'. Concordamos con la opinión de Senabre que a su vez está mucho más cercana a las propias declaraciones del propio Jesús Carrasco. Como señala Senabre, *Intemperie* se trata de una obra originalísima cuya reducción a una genealogía de influencias simplifica considerablemente lo que esta novela plantea. Frente al 'exceso' que anteriormente señalaba Pozuelo Yvancos como la 'cruz' de *Intemperie*, Senabre justo defiende, en línea con lo que hemos ido manteniendo en este artículo, que esta novela tiene 'tal precisión léxica, con tal detallismo que el lector tendrá en algunos momentos la sensación de estar redescubriendo la riqueza de un idioma límpido y sonoro, en el que cada objeto tiene su vocablo exacto' y Senabre añade en relación a lo que exponía al respecto que se trata de 'un idioma, por suerte, muy alejado del paupérrimo y repetitivo que, con muy pocas excepciones, los escritores actuales suelen utilizar'.

Si contraponemos las lecturas de Pozuelo Yvancos y Senabre, a mi juicio la óptica adoptada por el último es más acertada ya que tiene en cuenta que estamos ante otro tipo de novela completamente distinta a lo que ha sido hasta ahora la tónica general en autores españoles jóvenes actuales. En este sentido, Senabre incluso expondrá que 'como primera novela de un autor hasta ahora desconocido. *Intemperie* es una obra excepcional, que nos sumerge en el mundo de la mejor literatura'.

En esta línea de lectura y de interpretación presentada por Ricardo Senabre continuará la entrevista publicada por Nuria Azancot el 4 de febrero de 2013 también en las páginas de *El Cultural*. En ella, Jesús Carrasco comenta alguna de sus lecturas iniciales: '¿Quién me hizo escritor? Supongo que todo comenzó viendo a mi padre leer todas las tardes en su sillón. Mi vida lectora comenzó con Asterix. Mis primeros intentos literarios estuvieron alimentados por los relatos de Carver'. A continuación se repiten las mismas preguntas y temas de interés que hasta ahora había despertado *Intemperie*: '¿Por qué los personajes no tienen nombre (el chico, el pasto, el alguacil) y tampoco es posible identificar tiempo ni espacio?; Se ha escrito que el niño significa la inocencia, el pastor, el bien, y el alguacil el mal: ¿Es así como ve la realidad?; Los críticos han resaltado los vínculos de la novela con DeLillo, Delibes y Coetzee: ¿en qué aciertan y en qué se equivocan, qué le han prestado y qué no?' (Azancot, 4-2-2013). Carrasco, por su parte, continúa con la coherencia de su planteamiento inicial, ya expuesto en la entrevista con Fontana, al manifestar que:

> ¿Para qué ubicar la acción en un lugar o en otro? ¿Qué importa el topónimo, si el escenario está suficientemente trazado? [...] Mi visión de la realidad es más

> compleja. No me gustan los maniqueísmos, porque la experiencia me ha demostrado que la verdad, cuando existe, suele estar en los grises. [...] De los tres que cita, sólo reconozco a Coetzee como un referente en mi escritura. Su capacidad para penetrar con las palabras en las carnes del lector es altísima (Azancot, 4-2-2013).

Como podemos comprobar en los anteriores extractos, Carrasco sigue explicando que más que una genealogía de influencias son sus preferencias lectoras las que han podido conformar su educación literaria sin que eso tenga por qué ser el reflejo exacto de lo que leemos en *Intemperie*. La insistencia en el mismo tipo de preguntas, por parte del periodismo cultural del momento, denota la dificultad que la inmediata recepción de la crítica cultural tuvo para poder ofrecer a los lectores un conjunto de claves de lectura que no cayeran en el tópico. La imposibilidad de ubicar esta novela, debido a su originalidad, dentro de lo que se estaba publicando en este momento dejaba a los críticos en una difícil posición que ahora hemos visto que tan sólo Senabre supo solventar con amplitud de miras al celebrar en seguida la singularidad de esta novela de Jesús Carrasco.

El 4 de febrero de 2013 también encontramos en la prensa digital otro documento de interés para el análisis de la recepción inmediata de *Intemperie* que en esta ocasión es publicado en *El diario.es*. En esta nota titulada 'Intemperie: la quincuagésima Gran Novela del Año', Carlos González Peón hace un recorrido personal e impresionista por las reseñas que hasta ese momento habían aparecido en prensa en torno a *Intemperie*. Si bien el tono empleado por González Peón no es propio de la publicación en un medio de comunicación, también es cierto que expresa una reserva importante en torno a la manera en la que la crítica cultural se aproximó a la obra al indicar que 'habiendo tanto que mirar nos fijemos siempre en lo mismo dice bastante de nosotros como lectores y mucho también de algunos escritores' (González Peón, 4-2-2013). En su opinión, el hecho de que la crítica incida en los mismos aspectos a la hora de ofrecer un horizonte de referencias culturales sobre la novela subraya una cierta tendencia generalizada en los medios de comunicación a ensalzar o despreciar un texto literario sin siquiera haberlo leído como si todo ejercicio de lectura convergiera en torno a la 'necesidad de encontrar un mesías de las letras que recupere la gloria perdida hace tanto y nunca más encontrada'. Como hemos visto en las declaraciones del propio Jesús Carrasco, la escritura de *Intemperie*, lejos de una genealogía mesíanica, se encuentra enraizada en la elección de una estética y de un estilo narrativo sin referencias toponímicas, de líneas esenciales y de conflictos universales alejados de los referentes del modelo de ficción histórica propuesto por escritores como Javier Cercas, Isaac Rosa o Almudena Grandes que ha obtenido tanta atención por parte de lectores y críticos en los últimos veinte años.

También en febrero, el día 1, encontramos en las páginas del periódico *El País* un artículo firmado por Íñigo López Palacios con diversos extractos resultado de una entrevista con Jesús Carrasco. La nota es clarificadora porque en ella se le vuelve a preguntar a Carrasco sobre el tema recurrente de la genealogía de influencias, de manera todavía más concreta, sobre la presencia de Cormac McCarthy en *Intemperie* a lo que contesta que: 'Me entra un poco la risa con estas referencias. Si me pilla con 19 años, igual me permea, pero con 40 simplemente lo agradeces y entiendes que al no tener trayectoria previa es una forma de presentarme a aquellos que no me han leído. No lo veo como algo avieso, pero sí, se han pasado' (López Palacios, 1-2-2013). Y sobre la cuestión del estilo que otros críticos ya había tildado de exceso formalista, Jesús Carrasco declaraba que:

> Me interesan los temas de peso humano. Y esos tienden a ser milenarios, vienen desde la literatura arcaica y nos siguen interesando. Mi foco está ahí. En temas que considero trascendentes. Es mi forma de entender la vida. La relación del habitante de una ciudad con el teléfono móvil en 2013, por ejemplo, me parece algo más mutable, y por eso menos interesante. Pero no se contrapone a ningún tipo de literatura. Si tiene una forma clásica, o no, que lo juzguen otros. Los lectores, los críticos o quien corresponda (López Palacios, 1-2-2013).

Las palabras de Carrasco sobre este tema son muy claras. A Carrasco le interesan aquellos temas que transcienden lo estrictamente anecdótico, tal y como hemos podido comprobar con las anteriores palabras. Al mes siguiente, en marzo de 2013, apareció el número 149 de la revista *Mercurio*. En la página 18 de esta publicación encontramos una reseña firmada por Santos Sanz Villanueva cuyo título es 'Parábola de la dignidad'. Esta reseña se trata, a nuestro juicio, de la mejor y más completa noticia que fue publicada en prensa durante los meses de promoción de la novela. Ya resulta bastante significativo que frente al título de 'Cara y cruz de *Intemperie*' de Pozuelo Yvancos cuyo espíritu sancionador es evidente, nos hallamos frente al de 'Parábola de la dignidad' que se funde con la clave de lectura que Jesús Carrasco ya había ofrecido en entrevistas a varios medios. Sanz Villanueva intuyó inmediatamente que esta novela había empezado a sufrir los efectos de una recepción critica cultural que se encontraba completamente desubicada frente a lo que proponía la lectura de *Intemperie*: 'Efecto de enorme desconcierto produce *Intemperie*: tanto por el primitivismo ruralista extremo que nuclea el argumento como por el léxico inhabitual que tiende a robar buena parte de protagonismo al libro' (Sanz Villanueva, 2013). A continuación Sanz Villanueva destaca que los rasgos 'inusuales y llamativos' de esta obra 'encubren, sin embargo, una novela de aprendizaje desarrollada con la perspectiva infrecuente de la parábola'. Comparto plenamente la idea esbozada aquí por Sanz Villanueva. Nuestra lectura de *Intemperie* es la de encontrarnos frente a una parábola sobre la dignidad donde dos personajes, el niño y el viejo, conforman lo que Esther Peeren denomina en *The Spectral Metaphor* (2014) como 'spectral agency' a propósito de su estudio y que guarda un estrecho paralelismo con la forma en la que los personajes de *Intemperie* van corporeizándose a lo largo de la novela:

> After establishing how undocumented migrants, servants or domestic workers, mediums and missing persons manifest, in the literary texts, films and television analysed, as living ghosts associated with different aspects of the spectral metaphor and suffering varying degrees of dispossession, I explore whether and how these groups can find ways, individually or collectively, to acquire (a greater measure of) agency, so that hey, too, may live on (Peeren, 2014: 16).

Efectivamente, en *Intemperie* los personajes del niño y del viejo son personas que más que estar delimitadas psicológicamente hasta el detalle por el autor, se manifiestan como entidades ligeramente 'desenfocadas', usando la propia terminología de Carrasco, que se revelan a lo largo de las páginas de la novela al mismo tiempo que luchan contra diferentes modalidades de desposesión. La narración de *Intemperie* constituye, no sólo como Pozuelo Yvancos, Senabre o Sanz Villanueva destacaran al calificarla de 'novela de aprendizaje', ante todo una parábola cuya acción se articula en el pulso que los personajes mantienen con las posibilidades de adquirir visibilidad, en otras palabras, de tomar las riendas de su propio destino, de intervenir (en el sentido de 'agency') sobre las condiciones que configuran su propia presencia en la historia que es relatada.

Sanz Villanueva mantiene en su reseña que el uso de un léxico rural desaparecido tiene un 'prurito arcaizante' y que es un 'desacierto que se compensa, en cambio, con la magnífica capacidad para yuxtaponer el más crudo naturalismo y la más intensa sensibilidad lírica' (Sanz Villanueva, 2013: 18). Desde nuestra perspectiva, el uso de un léxico desaparecido concuerda precisamente con la manera en la que se articula la visibilidad de todo un mundo invisible que va encarnándose a través de la palabra para hacerle presente al lector la parábola espectral de desposesión en la que nos embarca la lectura de *Intemperie*. Sanz Villanueva concluirá que uno de los aciertos de la novela se encuentra en 'llevar al límite la descontextualización de la anécdota' (Sanz Villanueva, 2013: 18), a lo cual añadimos que este aspecto está especialmente logrado en la novela ya que una fábula sobre la desposesión del calado de *Intemperie* necesitaba que lo espectral cobrara fuerza frente a lo meramente referencial para así poder diluir lo concreto en lo universal.

La siguiente noticia de relevancia que encontramos en la prensa española nos lleva hasta las páginas de *La Crónica de Badajoz* del número correspondiente al 26 de mayo de 2013. La entrevista está firmada por Antonio Medina Díaz y lleva el título de 'Jesús Carrasco, escritor: "Creo que *Intemperie* es un fresco sobre la dignidad". En el artículo se aprecia como, casi medio año después de la publicación del libro, la crítica cultural española seguía estando desorientada sobre dónde ubicar esta novela de Jesús Carrasco tal y como Sanz Villanueva ya hemos visto que nos prevenía. En este sentido, el periodista escribía 'una novela que con apenas 200 páginas y tres personajes, tiene el aliento de un clásico: *Pedro Páramo*, *Cien años de soledad*, el mejor Delibes, el mejor Cela…' (Medina Díaz, 6-5-2013). La cuestión de la consolidación de una genealogía de influencias sigue siendo una cuestión fundamental para el periodismo cultural aunque el propio Jesús Carrasco ya llevara medio año explicando que en todo caso era una cuestión secundaria para acercarse a su novela. Ante la pregunta de qué es *Intemperie* el autor ahonda en la idea, repetida por él mismo en otros medios, de que se trata en todo caso de un fresco sobre la dignidad. Las otras dos preguntas, que ya hemos visto que se iban repitiendo en entrevista tras entrevista, tampoco faltan en esta: la ausencia de nombres propios y la influencia de Delibes. Desde luego las preguntas no destacan por su originalidad ni por su altura intelectual pero sí que nos demuestran que, a fuerza de abundar en los estereotipos que rodearon a la novela desde el primer momento, se asientan unas claves de lectura de la obra que configuran la primera lectura de *Intemperie* y que se sistematizan dentro de la crítica cultural.

De hecho no será hasta una entrevista publicada en *El País* con el título de 'Jesús Carrasco: "la obsesión actual por aprovechar el tiempo me parece atroz" fechada el 5 de agosto de 2013, cuando por fin encontremos en la prensa cultural del momento a un periodista que le pregunte directamente a Jesús Carrasco por el significado del concepto de dignidad en *Intemperie*:

> P: Ha dicho que el tema principal de su novela es la dignidad. ¿Por qué le interesa tanto ese concepto?
> R: La dignidad surge en cada esquina. Solo hay que verla, es como la belleza o el arte, y consiste en ser capaz de mantener la postura después de sufrir las inclemencias de la vida. Eso me interesa muchísimo, y quiero ser capaz de dirigir mi vida en esa dirección. Ser capaz de mantener la postura, de ser esa persona que en el metro, cuando alguien está siendo agredido, interviene (López Iturriaga, 5-8-2013).

Por tanto, teniendo en cuenta lo expuesto por el propio autor, parece bastante claro que la desorientación de parte del periodismo cultural se debía más a sus propios prejuicios lectores que a lo que Carrasco o el texto de la novela proponía y que tan sólo acertó a ver Sanz Villanueva al definir *Intemperie* como una parábola de la dignidad. Quizá por ello resulta aún más significativo el testimonio de Carrasco cuando Iturriaga, al preguntarle sobre la genealogía de influencias de *Intemperie*, le comente que 'Se ha relacionado su novela con el Delibes de *Los santos inocentes*, pero no tanto con *La familia de Pascual Duarte*, de Cela, el primer libro que me vino a la cabeza cuando empecé a leer Intemperie. ¿Es una referencia para usted?'. A lo que Carrasco contesta que ni esa obra ni el 'tremendismo' como movimiento literario son una referencia para él. Aunque, por otro lado, sí que reconoce el interés que le han despertado otros autores:

> R: He leído mucha más literatura norteamericana que española. Los relatos de Carver son durísimos, no se salva nadie, todo es atroz, y para que veas un hilito de esperanza! Al mismo tiempo son relatos poderosos, bien tramados, que te enganchan, y que a mí me transmiten muchas cosas. Cuando hablo de Carver, hablo de Richard Ford, de John Updike, de John Cheever o de Cormac McCarthy: si acaso, viene de ahí esta visión un poco lúgubre de la realidad. P: Supongo que su estilo, tan desnudo, también bebe de esos autores. R: Ahí yo creo que Carver es el campeón. Hay un cuento suyo que dice: "Un día llamaron a mi puerta y encontré un hombre con ganchos que quería vender una foto de mi casa". El cuento dura un poco más, pero por mí se podía haber acabado así. Él era el rey de la poda, y yo aspiro a ser no el rey ni el príncipe, pero sí a ser un buen podador. Quitar, quitar y quitar, y dejar interpretar a los demás.

Al final del anterior fragmento, Carrasco introduce el que es uno de los conceptos clave dentro del proceso de escritura de su obra: poda. Por tanto, nuestro autor pone en práctica un ejercicio de escritura en el que, lejos de la sumisión y adherencia a una genealogía de influencias, esencializa los tiempos, acciones, lugares y personajes que aparecen en el texto para que se hagan visibles para cada lector en su momento particular de acercamiento a la novela.

En este sentido, *Intemperie* se podría definir como una gran metáfora espectral sobre la dignidad cuyo estilo y técnica van encaminadas a que sea el lector el que tenga la posibilidad de dar cuerpo a las presencias que aparecen en esta novela. De ahí proviene la concisión y el interés por la palabra desnuda que Carrasco expresa, una y otra vez, en los meses de la inmediata recepción de la novela durante los cuales la crítica cultural se encontraba claramente desorientada ante la novedad que presentaba esta novela.

Ese cierto desamparo en cuanto a la recepción, únicamente subsanado por Sanz Villanueva y el propio Jesús Carrasco encuentra su espejo en la desposesión experimentada por el chico en la novela como así leemos en 'Quizá el desamparo que le había expulsado del hogar que Dios designó para él ya se había disipado por entonces' (Carrasco, 2013: 23). El estado de marginación de este sujeto en la novela tiene reminiscencias bíblicas que aparecen en la misma novela como así ocurre en 'la mujer de Lot viendo arder Sodoma' (Carrasco, 2013: 89) o en 'revolvía las hojas transparentes de la Biblia abierta sobre el suelo' (Casrrasco, 2013: 93). Esa Biblia transparente, espectral, es la propia narración principal en la que se ven envueltos estas presencias esencializadas que aquí preferimos denominar, siguiendo a Peeren (2014), como 'living ghosts' más que personajes. Continuas alusiones al culto religioso las encontramos en las páginas 154, 162, 176 y muestra su más claro ejemplo en la página 202 de la novela cuando leemos: 'Una densidad de sacristía vieja, donde los ropajes ceremoniales habían sido hilados en el comienzo mismo de los tiempos y donde las paredes habían absorbido, durante siglos, los gritos de los monaguillos, huérfanos y expósitos. El dolor y la caridad. La muerte arrumbada. La podredumbre abriéndose paso entre pecados inenarrables'. En este caso, la imposibilidad de contar, de explicar el horror, tan sólo es visible a través de la misma espectralidad de los hechos narrados y de sus protagonistas: el lector visibiliza en su imaginación la incorpórea presencia de otros chicos, encarnados en el niño de *Intemperie*, que también experimentaron el terror en aquellos muros. Sin duda una experiencia que encuentra refrendo en el final del libro cuando leemos: 'Luego volvió a la puerta y allí permaneció mientras duró la lluvia, mirando cómo Dios aflojaba por un rato las tuercas de su tormento' (Carrasco, 2013: 221). Parábola, metáfora espectral, reminiscencias bíblicas sobre la desposesión y el pecado, todos ellos son elementos que sin duda vertebran la escritura de *Intemperie* y en ellos se asienta y cobra lógica la utilización de un lenguaje que remite a un mundo rural desaparecido, también espectral, como así denotan términos como 'Albarda', 'Aparejo', 'Arroba', 'Destrabar', 'Serones', 'Trébede', 'Vaguada', expresiones como 'Con la tarde claudicando…' o 'Vas a ayudarme a dar portillo…' y fragmentos como 'Buscó en los serones una trenza de albardín que había sobrado del redil y la ató a la retranca…' (Carrasco, 2013: 80). Quizá para los críticos que no provengan de un contexto de experiencias reales y para la mayoría urbanita de los lectores esta sea una 'neolengua' pero la realidad es que este lenguaje formaba parte de una realidad cotidiana en las zonas rurales de España. Una realidad que efectivamente ha desaparecido y tan sólo se manifiesta de manera espectral en el recuerdo de aquellas personas que se formaron en ese mundo extinto y ahora en el imaginario de un público lector que aunque no capte en su totalidad el universo semántico que se nos propone, al menos sí es capaz, como así le sucedió a los críticos culturales que consolidaron la primera recepción de la novela, de apreciar la fuerza de un estilo que se aparta por completo del modelo de ficción histórica con enseñanza moral que se ha popularizado en nuestros días y que los estudiosos han venido a denominar como la 'novela de la memoria' (Valdivia, 2013).

Una de las preguntas que se repitió en los diferentes medios de prensa escrita fue la de ¿qué era *Intemperie*?. Jesús Carrasco explicó, en reiteradas ocasiones, que una definición era del todo innecesaria y que debían ser los lectores los que juzgaran particularmente cómo consideraban que la novela les interpelaba. En todo caso, Carrasco aludió a su novela como una 'exploración sobre la dignidad' o un 'fresco sobre la dignidad'. En ningún caso, como hemos comprobado, el autor intentó cerrar el sentido de la novela a una sola lectura y a una sola definición. Sin embargo, la crítica, en su mayoría desorientada ante una obra tan original por su propuesta narrativa, reacción ante su propia perplejidad intentando crear una genealogía de influencias que le permitiera encajar una obra que había tenido el efecto de desubicar a los críticos culturales. Salvo las excepciones de Sanz Villanueva y Senabre, el resto de críticos y de periodistas culturales tomaron al pie de la letra lo que había sido tan sólo una propuesta de lectura lanzada por parte de la editorial Seix Barral. El autor, en sus entrevistas, nos recuerda una y otra vez que no le interesan las influencias y que sus preferencias lectoras en todo caso se encuentran, como su propia voz biográfica, lo más diluidas posible en la narración hasta desaparecer.

Nuestro estudio sobre la recepción de *Intemperie* se cierra con una nota final publicada en *El País*. El 18 de diciembre de 2013. *Intemperie* acababa de ser elegida, según los lectores de este periódico, como la mejor novela del año. La nota está firmada por el propio Carrasco:

> Hace unas semanas, tras la clausura de las Jornadas de Bibliotecas de Extremadura, un hombre vino a verme

> y me dijo que él era el niño de *Intemperie*. Tuve que mirarlo a los ojos para comprender lo que quería decirme. Tenía una mirada profunda y apesadumbrada. Charlar con él me confirmó lo que intuía en sus ojos: que había sufrido, que se había rozado con la vida, que tenía cicatrices por todas partes. Me confesó que el libro le había dolido pero que también lo había sanado. Yo no sé muy bien por qué escribo, pero ese encuentro me ayudó a comprender dónde reside el poder de la literatura y, más ampliamente, de la palabra. Antes de comenzar una novela, sabemos que lo que vamos a encontrar es un artefacto. Un montón de palabras sobre un papel en blanco. Sin embargo, durante la lectura, suspendemos aquellas categorías que nos sirven para habitar el mundo y, por unas horas, nos desplazamos por un territorio que es, a lo sumo, sólo una imagen de la vida. ¿Por qué entonces a ese hombre le dolía una mera representación de lo real? La respuesta a esa pregunta bien vale un oficio y, para mí, condensa lo vivido en un año entero (Carrasco, 18-12-2013).

La anterior reflexión de Carrasco nos habla sobre el mismo carácter espectral de la literatura en general y de *Intemperie* en particular. Un hombre se había sentido identificado con el personaje del niño hasta presentarse como el 'niño de *Intemperie*'. Esta visibilización del trauma, del horror, tiene un carácter espectral porque le da la posibilidad a historias de manifestarse y de tomar cuerpo en ese 'montón de palabras sobre un papel en blanco'. Esta nota de Carrasco cerraba la recepción de la novela y nos muestra una divergencia entre lo que parte de la crítica cultural ha explicado por un lado y lo que el autor ha expuesta y el público lector ha experimentado por otro. Ese destiempo ha tenido sus raíces en un acercamiento crítico a la novela en la que en algunas ocasiones se ha tratado de amoldar el texto a las categorías literarias puestas en alza en una coyuntura determinada sin tener en cuenta la radical especificidad de la novela. *Intemperie*, ya traducida a más de ocho lenguas y constituida en un claro éxito lector en medio mundo, requiere una mirada desprejuiciada en el que el espectro de la literatura se conjura en forma de una 'imagen de la vida' tal y como Jesús Carrasco nos advertía. Quizá hoy más que nunca sería necesario hacerse eco de aquello que Borges nos recordaba en su fundamental reflexión 'El escritor argentino y la tradición', cuando afirmaba que: 'Platón dijo que los poetas son amanuenses de un dios, que los anima contra su voluntad, contra sus propósitos, como el imán anima a una serie de anillos de hierro' (Borges, 1997). Por tanto, podemos concluir que la configuración de una genealogía de influencias en el estudio de una novela como *Intemperie* es una golosa tentación que el crítico cultural debería, como mínimo, aplicar con sumo cuidado.

Obras Citadas

Azancot, N. (4-2-2013). 'Jesús Carrasco' en *El Mundo*.

Borges, J. L. (1997). 'El escritor argentino y la tradición' en *Discusión,* Madrid, Alianza.

Carrasco, J. (2013). *Intemperie,* Barcelona, Seix Barral.

___. (18-12-2013). 'Mejor novela de 2013, según los lectores de El País: *Intemperie*' en *El País*.

Europa Press (21-12-2012). 'Seix Barral publica *Intemperie*, debut literario de Jesús Carrasco.

Fontana, A. (19-1-2013). 'Jesús Carrasco escritor: "*Intemperie* es un western ibérico"' en *El Mundo*.

___ (22-1-2013). 'Jesús Carrasco: "Intemperie" es un western ibérico' en *ABC*.

González Peón, C. (4-2-2013). 'Intemperie: la quincuagésima Gran Novela del Año' en *Eldiario.es*.

La Opinión de Málaga (13-10-2012). 'Jesús Carrasco, el escritor español desconocido que está triunfando en Fráncfort'.

López Iturriaga, M. (5-8-2013). 'Jesús Carrasco: "La obsesión actual por el tiempo me parece atroz"' en *El País*.

López Palacios, Í. (1-2-2013). 'Revelación literaria a los 40' en *El País*.

Medina Díaz, A. (6-5-2013). 'Jesús Carrasco, escritor: "Creo que 'Intemperie' es un fresco sobre la dignidad"' en *La Crónica de Badajoz*.

Niño, V. M. (26-5-2013). 'Jesús Carrasco, un narrador tan sobrio como su *Intemperie*' en *El Norte de Castilla*.

Peeren, E. (2014). *The spectral metaphor: living ghosts and the Agency of Invisibility,* Palgrave Macmillan, London.

Pozuelo Yvancos, J. M. (19-1-2013). 'Cara y cruz de Jesús Carrasco' en *El Mundo*.

Sanz Villanueva, S. (2013). 'Parábola de la dignidad' en *Mercurio*, nº149, marzo, 18.

Senabre, R. (18-1-2013). 'Intemperie' en *El Mundo*.

Valdivia, P. (2013). *Sefarad* de Antonio Muñoz Molina (estudio, edición y notas de P. Valdivia), Madrid, Cátedra.

Epilogue: algorithms and disinherited literature

What is an algorithm? A set of precise specifications on how to solve a class of problems. We tend to confuse algorithms with Artificial Intelligence, and this with machine learning but they are all different elements. Algorithms can be very useful to detect and to understand anomalies. At this current stage of my book, the reader has a better idea on some of the spectres that populate the Spanish literature anomaly presented here.

In this regard, I find it is not enough with spotting anomalies, deconstruct them and expose their mechanisms. I believe it is crucial to propose alternatives. A regular principle in Physics: the gap left in the space by an object that has been displaced tends to be filled with another object. In other words, if we crash the traditional literary canon a new hierarchy will raise. Consequently, I believe that the traditional Spanish canon should be undermined, studied, understood, shaken but not utterly removed because the readings its produced have informed audiences and, thus, their ways of approaching the texts.

What I find more valuable is to awake the self-awareness of the communities of readers and to empower them with critical tools that can provide them with both autonomy and agency. I want them (this is something I always repeat in my classes) to be independent and set up their criteria and not simply replace a theological-anomaly (the Spanish Literary Canon) by another theological-anomaly of any kind. Readers need, metaphorically, algorithms which can assist them to enrich their cultural imaginary.

My contribution to empower readers is fourfold: 1) I have demonstrated that only the transnational intellectual and cultural matrix can protect us from the nationalist appropiation of culture for political and power interests; 2) Literature is in itself a crisis practice and it has the potentiality to unfold contraditcions and patterns normativized in institutional discourse as it is the only human discourse that masters other discourses; 3) Literature has an autonomous spectral agency which escapes any attempts to reduce its meaning to set fixed a priori: it can be invisibilized but not destroyed as it manifests in the cracks of instutional canonicity; 4) Invisibilized works do not struggle to be part of the institutional canon (which indicates academic practices of replacement but not of empowerment) but to gain autonomy as disinherited literature.

The latest is a crucial point I would like to clarify and expand here. For a cultural object to be out of the Canon does not mean that its symbolic capital charge equals zero. However, it implies to have a different symbolic capital charge as it vibrates under the frequency of the Canon but on a different set of specifications, to keep using my original metaphor, on a different algorithm.

In my view, a literary practice falls into what I define as 'disinherited literature' when a) it establishes a conflictive relationship with the institutional canon as raison d'être, b) it needs the existence of a traditional canon to define its specificity *ex negativo*, c) it experiences a double displacement which ultimately signifies its spectral condition. We have seen several cases in this book: Morales, Encina, Cervantes, Lorca, Carrasco, among others.

Also, it is important to note that not all the works written by an author should/can be under the coordinates of the notion of 'disinherited literature'. The mechanism is far subtler. A work can be part of 'disinherited literature' during some time until a new algorithm becomes more powerful and replaces a pre-existent one. Or an author can suffer a spectral state during a period of his production, gain visibility and move again to a spectral position. Or even what is more interesting: an author/work can be spectral and be unconsciously accepted as this by the institutional canon.

There is a definitory pattern in all works and authors belonging to the category of 'disinherited literature': they are transnational, and the meaning of their works has been modified in connection to the difficulty of fitting and appropriating their cultural innovations for justifying political and power strategies. In this regard, 'disinherited' is not a term with a negative connotation. To the contrary, 'disinherited' is the condition of existence of those works that have resisted to become part of a grand nationalist narrative.

To sum it up, the algorithm of the 'disinherited literature' allow us not only to see the invisible but also to embrace it, to understand it in its radical particularities and, what is even more important, it enhances a reading that does not modify the text in its interaction by the observer. This careful reading of the works stays at the moment created by the texts, and it does not twist the work to say what our political or cultural conjuncture wants us to read in them.

As indicated in the earlier pages of this book, I believe there is a new wave in Literary Studies which has begun to flourish. This new school is sorting out the methodological problem of the excess of subjective speculation by using empirical methodologies which allow us to tackle specific research questions. To my understanding, impressionistic speculative approaches almost killed Literary Studies while also funded many fake academic positions.

The re-foundation of Philology (in its both diachronic and synchronic directions) together with a New Positivism it is opening a new field of transboundary Literary Studies whose results we start just to scratch from the surface. A transnational multidisciplinary approach will not only enrich particular readers uses of literature but also will open up to address the big questions of our times: Is it possible to develop an artificial consciousness? What is the role of national canonicity in the era of the-internet-of-all things? How can a machine learning spot or deal with cultural differences and universals? How can we emotionally cope with the new world of social relations emerging under the Globalization process? These are some of the challenges and questions we cannot wait to give an answer, or somebody else will do it for us with, perhaps, undesirable results. Literary scholars are privileged by training to reply to these questions because they are experts in the field which primarily feeds literature and ultimately life in its variety of representations: the unique and compelling realm of human imagination.

INDEX

Hispanic Transnational Studies
edited by Prof. Dr. Pablo Valdivia (University of Groningen)

Robert Folger; José Elías Gutiérrez Meza (Eds.)
La mirada del otro en la literatura hispánica
Este conjunto de trabajos examina la representación del otro en distintas expresiones de la Literatura Hispánica: novela, teatro, memoria, zarzuela, relato de viajes, entre otras. Asimismo, se sigue una perspectiva diacrónica que abarca desde la literatura del Siglo de Oro español hasta la literatura latinoamericana más actual.
Bd. 4, 2017, 304 S., 34,90 €, br., ISBN 978-3-643-90766-0

Manuel Aznar Soler
El teatro de Jorge Semprún
Jorge Semprún, escritor y militante del Partido Comunista de España hasta su expulsión en 1965, es mucho más conocido como novelista, ensayista o guionista cinematográfico que como autor teatral. Sin embargo, es autor de cinco obras dramáticas que se analizan en este libro: Soledad, obra inédita escrita hacia 1947 en lengua francesa; *¡Libertad para los 34 de Barcelona!*, obra en un acto publicada clandestinamente en la España franquista de 1953; *Le retour de Carole Neher*, escrita en francés, estrenada en 1995 y publicada en 1998; *Gurs. Una tragedia europea*, inédita, escrita en tres lenguas distintas (alemán, castellano y francés); y, por último, *Moi, Éléanore, fille de Karl Marx, juive!*, publicada póstumamente en 2014.
Bd. 1, 2016, 312 S., 29,90 €, br., ISBN 978-3-643-90589-5

LIT Verlag Berlin – Münster – Wien – Zürich – London
Auslieferung Deutschland / Österreich / Schweiz: siehe Impressumsseite